Livret numl
Series: Of Islands a

C000019098

Madei

Of Islands and Women

Madeira

Women, History, Books and Places

SUSANNA HOE

HOLO BOOKS
THE WOMEN'S HISTORY PRESS
OXFORD

Published in 2004 by The Women's History Press
A division of HOLO Books
Clarendon House
52 Cornmarket, Oxford OX1 3HJ

British Library Cataloguing in Publication Data
A catalogue record for this book is available from the British Library

ISBN 0–9537730–8–6

10   9   8   7   6   5   4   3   2   1

Designed and produced for HOLO Books by
Chase Publishing Services, Fortescue, Sidmouth EX10 9QG, England
Printed and bound in the European Union

In memory of my mother, Johanna Fox Hoe
1920–2002
Whose visit to Madeira with us in 2001 was so happy.

Contents

List of Illustrations

Preface

Madeira

'Where will I be when the belladonnas open? Whence will the soft scent of the azaleas evoke my yearning?' wrote Luísa Grande whose penname was Luzia. Born in Lisbon, brought up in Madeira, flitting as an adult between the two places, her writing constantly evokes what the Portuguese call *saudades* (memories or longing).

In all places there are separate worlds living side by side. Often you are brought up short when you catch a glimpse of one of those that have been hitherto hidden. Is it possible to enter Luzia's world, when she was so torn herself, particularly when you don't speak or read Portuguese? Probably not. But this book, the work of a stranger, does its best; for Madeira beguiles us all. In drawing on written sources, though, the more accessible accounts of other outsiders, those who come from my world, inevitably predominate.

Today, many travellers to this now autonomous region of Portugal still go for the winter sun, the magnificent walks, the tropical and temperate gardens dating back more than a hundred years, the glorious wild flowers and trees, and distinctive mountain views. Less well-known is the history of Madeira's women, from slaves and lepers to privileged British expatriates and Portuguese noblewomen; and most of the writing of women travellers and residents – books, reminiscenses, diaries and letters – has been overlooked.

In the nineteenth century, people visited the island in the hope that the dry, warm winter might help them to recover from illness – usually consumption (tuberculosis). By coincidence, we went there for the first time in the winter of 2001 when I was still suffering the after-effects of illness. We not only saw Madeira through historical lenses but were more limited than usual in what I could achieve. Aware of the gaps we had to leave then, which became more obvious the more I learnt, we returned in the spring of 2004 so that I could experience Madeira with more joy and so finish my research. I hope I have captured a flavour of all these elements in this offering to the visitor or armchair traveller, and even the resident.

Series – 'Of Islands and Women'

The places most alluring to travellers or holiday makers are often islands. But even the small ones may have too much to see in one visit. Over the years I have, therefore, refined a stratagem that begins to overcome that problem.

And, since I assume that others, particularly women, may like to travel as I do, I put forward the following proposition: the most rewarding way for a woman to visit an island is to read books by women who have travelled there, or by or about women who have been part of its history, and to visit the places they describe or where they had their being. Happily, the novelty and excitement of the chase seems to appeal as much to my husband, Derek Roebuck, as to me.

Guide books, and those travelling companions which include extracts from travellers to a particular place, offer essential or pleasing information about many aspects, but seldom much about women. I have had to do most of my own research from scratch and, with Derek's help, find the places. Since we have now travelled our way so often, it seems natural to write about it – to fill a gap. Hence this series and, as the books are intended to be quite short and portable, I have revived the word 'livret'.

The subtitle common to each, 'Women, History, Books and Places', combines the essential elements of the series. There are suggestions for which books to read, as well as a flavour of them, and where to go. A historical background, concentrating as far as possible on women, is followed by itineraries. Most of the information comes from women's accounts or studies and our own experiences.

You may feel that what follows is sufficient for your reading needs about the island in question. But for those who share, or would like to share, my book obsession, this is my method. Some of the books I read before I go, some I read there, and some I read on my return. As far as possible, I like to have my own copies. This has become much easier now that you can buy secondhand books on the internet, and I have suggested which books should be easy to come by and which not. That is not to say that I don't visit bookshops: to do so invites serendipity.

A list of future livrets – about islands that have already been visited – is at the front of this one. If you have ideas for them that you think should be included, please let me know; I hope that your story, properly acknowledged, might form part of the text. In that way we can extend the boundaries of what is known about women's past and have some fun.

Oxford
August 2004

Author's Note

As so often happens where more than one language is involved, spelling consistency is a problem. The first governor of Porto Santo was from Genoa and arrived called Perestrello but, like many who settled in Madeira, he became Portuguese, Perestrelo. Where Italian consonants tend to be double, Portuguese are single. The same applies to English and Portuguese. Thus the Portuguese Lazareto usually becomes Lazaretto in English quotations. I use the single consonant in my own text. In Portuguese, Elizabeth is Isabel; in that language you may read, for example, Empress Isabel of Austria for the woman English speakers call Elizabeth.

Most English-speakers today call the inhabitants of Madeira 'Madeirans', as did most nineteenth century travellers. But some twentieth century writers, and some families of British extraction long resident in Madeira, insist on the Portuguese '*Madeirenses*' (pronounced Madder-ehnss). Although the latter users have made me feel self-conscious, I have decided to make it easy and use 'Madeirans'.

Confusion is caused by different facts or dates being adopted by different recorders of Madeira's history. I have had to plump for one version or the other – the one that my instinct and experience suggest is the more likely. Where possible I have done further research. Most families historically were not only intertwined by marriage, but extended as well. Many who appear here had several houses or quintas (properties), often more than one in town and more than one in the country. The history of many quintas has been lost, or mistaken facts perpetuated. Confusion has occurred over time and I'm not sure that I have always resolved it. Sometimes I have had the nerve to question received wisdom. Where possible I have tried out my theories. I have not wanted to burden you too much with the intricacies; on the other hand, nor do I want to misdirect you. Watch out, often streets and places are not marked consistently on maps and it is not possible for me to produce maps here that overcome that problem, except in words. I hope I have made it clear which places are private and which can be visited. When in doubt, err on the side of discretion.

The editor of Isabella de França's journals raises a question about the illustrations he uses, and which I have used too, courtesy of the Frederico de Freitas Museum where the originals are kept. Were the paintings really by her? I do not see how they could have been by anyone else, except perhaps her husband, since they often depict scenes personal to them. At one stage in her journal she wishes there was someone who could paint the scene. My conclusion was that she did it later from her written description and memory; I then happily found that the museum assumes she painted them. They may not be brilliant paintings technically but they are most evocative and as warm and quirky as her writing.

With so many characters involved in this livret, often women visitors who left written accounts which are interspersed with each other, it is not always easy to follow who is who and when. To help, there is a chronology at the end. Where in the nineteenth century women writers used titles, when I know their first name I tend to use it, often by itself. It seems more friendly. However, the honorific Dona was historically used for Portuguese women, certainly of the upper class, and this is sometimes the only way to distinguish the gender of names in Portuguese texts. As a cross-cultural courtesy, I have usually retained it. Women's names are in bold lettering when it is the only mention of them or when that occasion gives their fullest biographical details; bold page numbers in the index match that.

There are no footnotes but I have tried to make it clear not only where each quotation comes from, but also, in the case of diary entries, the date. I also suggest, when practical, the provenance of background information. The bibliography is divided into works by or about women, and those used for reference.

Portuguese informants in Madeira have been generous in providing me with material in Portuguese – a language in which I can only spot names and obvious words. My linguistically talented husband has done his best to draw appropriately from these sources. I am still conscious of the lack of names of individual country and working class women.

This is not intended to be a comprehensive guide book of Madeira; it is mainly about women and it is quite personal. You may well need an up-to-date companion guide as well. Some suggestions are in the bibliography. Get the latest maps too.

Acknowledgements

When I wrote the first draft of this book, I knew no one in Madeira except Martinho Macedo, the driver who so expertly introduced us to areas of his island on our first trip, and then on our second. That draft suffered from that lack and was rather different from this.

During the intervening years and particularly during our second visit, the contribution made by people in Madeira, and those outside familiar with it and its history, has been so substantial that it is impossible to thank them adequately. Some have also read the whole manuscript and some have read those parts to which they contributed; but they are in no way responsible for any remaining flaws. I am most grateful for that added help.

It would be invidious to single anyone out – everyone has been so hospitable, patient and informative, and given me so much of their time. These thanks are, therefore, in alphabetical order: João Carlos Almada (British Cemetery), Maria Helena Araújo (Vicentes Photographic Museum), Dr Shirley Ardener, Philippe Bettencourt (Frederico de Freitas Museum), Maria-Luísa Bianchi, Adam Blandy, Auriol Blandy, Christina Blandy, John Blandy, Louisa Blandy, staff of the Bodleian Library, Anne Evans Bohme, Rodney Bolt, Deirdre

Borges, João Borges, Gabrielle Bourn (Minet Library, Lambeth), Staff of the British Library, Dr Ros Burnett, Dr José Augusto Carvalho (Botanical Gardens), Dr Ana Margarida Camacho (Director, Frederico de Freitas Museum), Alan Chedzoy, Dr Francisco Clode, John Cossart, Mimi Dias, Dr Paulo de Freitas, Sister Edith (Franciscan Sisters of Our Lady of Victories), Emília Faria, John Farrow, Nancy Ferraz, Betty Garton, Guida Garton, Clare Gittings, Lord Grantley, Dr Dorothy O. Helly, Cecilia Jesus, Sister Kirilia (Franciscan Sisters of Our Lady of Victories), Luíza Leacock, Elizabeth Leeson, staff of the London Library, Louise McArron (National Library of Scotland), Della Maddison, Christopher Blandy Martin, Jean Marc Michel (Reid's Palace), Anthony Miles, Philippe Moreau (Choupana Hills Resort and Spa), Dr Teresa Pais (Director, Quinta das Cruzes Museum), Simon Phelps, Laura Ponsonby, Isabel de Portugal (Reid's Palace), Paul Roebuck, Lena Rymer-Rythen (Reid's Palace), Ana Kol Rodrigues (Quinta das Cruzes Museum), David Rutherford, Susan Seldon, Ana Vieira Soares, Dr Amândio de Sousa (Quinta das Cruzes Museum), Murray Symonds, Professor Alberto Vieira, Otilia Welsh, Jeanie Reid Wood, Coraline de Wurstemberger, Emília Zino, Jeremy Zino.

Ray Addicott could have been first in that list but needs special mention for seeing this book through the production process with his usual patience, flair and efficiency.

I cannot put my husband, Derek Roebuck, in alphabetical order. He has been with me every step, and not just in Madeira. His contribution is, as always, incalculable.

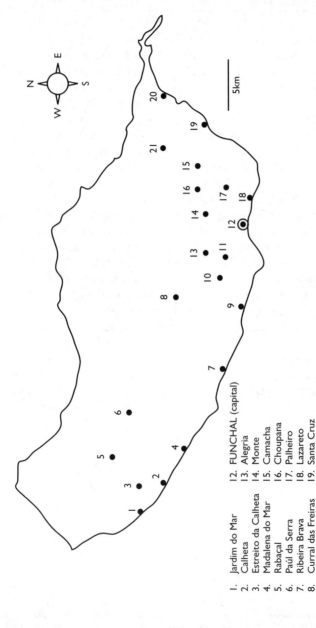

1. Jardim do Mar
2. Calheta
3. Estreito da Calheta
4. Madalena do Mar
5. Rabaçal
6. Paúl da Serra
7. Ribeira Brava
8. Curral das Freiras
9. Câmara de Lobos
10. Santana
11. São Roque
12. FUNCHAL (capital)
13. Alegria
14. Monte
15. Camacha
16. Choupana
17. Palheiro
18. Lazareto
19. Santa Cruz
20. Machico
21. Santo da Serra

Places in the Itineraries

Women's History

Anna d'Arfet and Machico

Some time in the fourteenth century, possibly when Philippa of Lancaster was consort of João I of Portugal, the runaway English lovers Anna d'Arfet and Robert Machim were driven by storm onto the east coast of an island in the Atlantic, not far from the north coast of Africa.

Their story may be a myth, but this is the gist: Anna was a noblewoman and heiress whom Robert, a merchant venturer, was deemed unfit to marry. She was, therefore, betrothed, or married, against her will, to an older man of her station; Robert was imprisoned. He escaped and they eloped in his ship from Bristol, hoping to find sanctuary in France. But contrary winds drove them further south-west and, after 13 days, they found refuge from the elements on a deserted shore rising to high mountains and thick forest. A few days later, during another storm, their ship slipped its anchor and sank. Anna, weakened by exposure, exertion and the loss of the ship, died in Robert's arms. Consumed by grief and guilt, he followed her.

The crew buried the couple, as they had promised, under a Christian monument and, building a raft, escaped from the inhospitable island. Their story eventually reached Prince Henry the Navigator of Portugal, son of Queen Philippa. He sent out an expedition under João Gonçalves Zarco and in 1420 Zarco, too, landed at a place he later called Machico (ostensibly after Anna and Robert Machim). The existence of what is now Madeira ('Wooded Land') became common knowledge and part of Portuguese territory, together with Porto Santo, the small island 35 miles to the north-east which had been 'discovered' the previous year.

1. 'The Tomb of Anna d'Arfet', as imagined by Mrs Bennett (possibly Anna Maria Bennett, c.1750–1808, novelist); from Bowles, *The Spirit of Discovery*, 1809

Two contrary impressions remain of the initial landing at Machico: while early Portuguese historians write of Anna d'Arfet and Robert Machim's adventures and tragedy as fact – Madeira thus owing its discovery to an English couple – nineteenth and twentieth century English visitors in their published accounts of Madeira tend to downplay or deny it, though giving many details of it taken from the Portuguese as they do so. Lady Emmeline Stuart-Wortley, for example, calls the story 'fabulous'. Edith Hutcheon, a believer, in *Things Seen in Madeira* (1928) provides a ready list of Portuguese sources. Lady Susan Harcourt's husband claims that Zarco called his first anchorage 'Porto dos Inglezes'.

Whatever the truth of Anna d'Arfet (Darbey, or Dorset or of Hereford) and Robert Machim (or à Machin) – and even the dates of their landfall at Madeira (and who was on the throne where) are at odds – the fishing port and administrative centre of Machico is worth a visit; you will find further details in the section 'From Funchal Eastwards' (pp. 43–6).

Women's History

Although early historical sources suggest knowledge of Madeira, no prehistoric remains have been found, nor any sign of pre-fourteenth century indigenous inhabitants so, with the story of Anne d'Arfet, the history of the islands is off to a late but womanly start. In what follows, some of the places connected with women, like Machico, form part of particular itineraries; others are elaborated as historical women are chronologically introduced. Books, unpublished records and their women authors permeate all sections.

Constança Rodrigues (c.1400–c.1495)

After Zarco and his companion, Tristão Vaz, had taken Madeira for Portugal, the island was divided diagonally between the two men as Captains (governors). Zarco took the south-western half, including what is now Funchal ('Place of Fennel'), and his wife Dona Constança Rodrigues de Almeida joined him there. She came from a rich family, he from a poor; in about 1414 he had eloped with her, his boss's daughter, and fled to Lisbon for the King's protection. In the 1450s, Zarco and Constança built a house where now stands the Quinta das Cruzes Museum (see also pp. 97–107). It was rebuilt more than once in the centuries that followed – the museum's structure dates from the eighteenth century – and all that remains of the original are some rescued monuments in the garden.

Four young Portuguese noblemen were brought over to marry the daughters of Constança and Zarco and given land on which to establish the first noble families. Other members of the Portuguese nobility followed, to be joined by merchants and adventurers from all over Europe. Their estates, particularly sugar, were worked by imported slaves and incoming landless settlers. There were nearly 3,000 slaves – from North Africa (Moors), West Africa and the Canaries – by the middle of the sixteenth century. Slavery was abolished in Portuguese territories in 1773.

The first children recorded as born on the island were twins born in 1425 to the wife of Gonçallo Ayres Ferreira who christened them Eve and Adam. There seem to be no records of their mother's name, and apparently no speculation about it, though the father's pedigree is established. The girl, known historically as **Eva Gomes**, was to marry Vasco Fernandes. In 1470, the twins built a chapel on the site of what is now Nossa Senhora do Monte ('Church of Our Lady of the Hill') at the summit of Monte. (See also 'Flowers, Gardens and Walks', p. 145)

Constança Rodrigues was responsible in 1425 for building the Santa Catarina Chapel overlooking Funchal's harbour. It was originally in wood but rebuilt in stone in the fifteenth and seventeenth centuries and is the oldest place of worship in Madeira. It became a museum but is now unused, sad and locked in the Santa Catarina Gardens (see p. 61). Dona Constança may have been an active participant in the development of the island: the first record of the leasing of a property, in 1484, is in her name.

There is some disagreement about the founding by one of Constança's grandchildren of the Santa Clara Convent (the Poor Clares) just below the Quinta das Cruzes Museum on Calçada de Santa Clara (then still the Zarco family home). One of our travellers, Ellen Taylor, attributes it to her granddaughter **Dona Constança de Noronha** in 1492 and adds that the first abbess was **Dona Isabel.** A more scholarly source attributes the direction, rather than the founding, first to Dona Isabel and adds that she was joined by her sisters Dona Constança and **Dona Elvira** who were already nuns. All were granddaughters of Constança and daughters of her son Captain João Gonçalves da Câmara and **Maria de Noronha**. Different sources suggest that the convent was founded either by Constança's son, or grandson Simon, in 1488 or 1496.

It is said elsewhere that the sisters became nuns because they could not find men who met their exacting standards but, since at least two of them had come from a convent in Portugal, it may be no reflection on the choice available in Madeira. It is clear that not all descendants of the founders of Madeira lived there all the time. Another grandson of Constança, Pedro, was married to **Dona Joana d'Eça** who was lady-in-waiting to Catherine of Braganza, probably in Portugal and when she was Queen of England (see p. 10). The couple also founded a chapel in Madeira. See pp. 90–7 for further details of the Santa Clara Convent.

Another convent, the Incarnation, founded in 1665 at the bottom of the Monte Road, was added to and finished by **Dona Isabel Maria Acciaiouli**. The church is still there in Calçada da Encarnacão. **Dona Isabel de França** founded the Mercês, a Capucin order, in 1654. I suspect that the husband of Isabella de França, an Englishwoman who visited Madeira in 1853, was of the same family. Isabella was to write that 'There are three convents of nuns still remaining though no novices are now allowed to enter. Two of them are large piles of building, but with no pretentions to Architecture.' There is a drawing of the Incarnation by Mary Young on p. 106. The founding of convents and chapels by rich women, and the religious and charitable activities they imply, has an added significance: while the inmates of convents were often there against their will, founding them and then embellishing them were acts of patronage, power and, even, creativity in an otherwise constrained life. Even where the buildings and institutions no longer exist, some of the commissioned art is in the Museum of Sacred Art in Funchal (see pp. 109–10).

Felipa Moniz

Christopher Columbus visited Madeira three times, the first, in 1478, staying with Bartolomeu Perestrelo, Captain of Porto Santo. The first Captain Bartolomeu Perestrelo came from Lombardy and had three wives. By the third, **Dona Isabella Moniz**, he had a son bearing his name and succeeding him as Captain, and a daughter, Felipa Perestrelo e Moniz, whom Columbus married. Their son was born in Madeira, according to those who wish Columbus to be part of its history. Some accounts discuss the location of their house (or houses) in Funchal. But Lady Emmeline Stuart-Wortley says it was demolished just before her visit in 1851 and Elizabeth Nichols suggests that this happened just before 1939. Noel Cossart, whose mother was descended from Perestrelo, claims, writing in 1984, that Columbus' 'palace' stood between Rua do Sabão and Rua da Esmeralda and that, at the time of his writing, a wall and one window remained. Today there is certainly a Praça do Colombo uniting those streets and some suggest that the Sugar Museum, *Cidade do Açucar*, is on the site but, since Felipa died in 1480 and the house was apparently built in 1494, I suspect it is a wild goose chase as far as women's history is concerned. But it was watching how the driftwood and debris floated off his wife's home island, Porto Santo, that eventually (1485) led Columbus to sail westwards towards what is now America; indeed, one account suggests that he married Felipa to get hold of her family's charts and logbooks. The Columbus House (museum) in Vila Baleiro, Porto Santo, is a more likely place to imagine Felipa, though there is no evidence there of her life.

Felipa the Prophet

Another Felipa (or Phelippa) of Porto Santo, the 17-year-old niece of Fernando Nunes, also has her place in Madeira's history. In 1533, uncle and niece declared themselves prophets and gained followers when Felipa, who had previously been paralysed, was able to walk. The cult, including members of the clergy, grew so strong that first the Madeira authorities, and then the Portuguese, became alarmed and sent a magistrate over to nip it in the bud. At least one account tells how the two leaders were taken to Machico to be tried. There they were displayed outside the church (which one is not mentioned) with lighted tapers in their hands and a placard round their necks – 'Prophets of Porto Santo' – while a mass was said inside. Felipa, whose apparent cure was permanent, married soon after and spent the rest of her life in Portugal.

Curral das Freiras (Nuns' Fold)

In 1566 the threat to Madeira's stability was more serious when some 1,000 French freebooters raided Funchal for its gold and silver. They stayed for two weeks, killed some 200 inhabitants and took what they could, including young girls. The population of the whole island was then only about 8,000, including 3,000 slaves. The raid prompted the nuns of Santa Clara to withdraw into the mountains to the north and find refuge in a valley known now as the Grand Curral or the Curral das Freiras (Nuns' Fold) – land given in the 1490s to the granddaughters of Constança Rodrigues who founded the convent. As Isabella de França explains, '[It] is a deep valley enclosed on all sides by precipices, as a cattle fold is by hurdles.' The refugees stayed there for about two months.

Sarah Bowdich visited the Grand Curral in 1823 and produced drawings, particularly of its rock formations; the one shown here is a part of its extraordinary panorama. Sarah will be discussed in more detail later (see Frederico de Freitas Museum, pp. 86–9). The Nuns' Fold is best described in words in her husband's book, edited by her after his death and obviously bearing her stamp, and her description suggests that the two of them entered the Curral as the nuns did in 1566, along the bed of the Ribeira dos Socorridos ('River of the Rescued' – not after the nuns but two officers of Zarco who got into trouble):

Having reached the bed of the torrent, we look around and feel as if we were in an amphitheatre of unscalable rocks without a single outlet ... the small valley, through which a few miserable huts are thinly scattered, presents flourishing vineyards and

2. Curral das Freiras by Sarah Bowdich, 1823, from Bowdich, *Excursions in Madeira*

smiling gardens of cabbages, pumpkins and sweet potatoes ... This is the highest point at which the vine is cultivated in Madeira, for making wine, and its success is entirely owing to the nuns of Santa Clara (to whom the Coural belongs) having given up their share of the profits, to their tenants, for the first seven years.

While the Bowdichs seem to have approached the Curral from below, most of their successors see it from the top. Emily Smith, in her unpublished diary, gives a detailed description on 26 November 1841 of how you got there:

We passed the Church of St António and numberless Vineyards and by a good road till we came to the halting place where I got into my Hammock and then the roughness of the road began & winding up & down the sides of lofty ridges forming the sides of the grand ravines, with their rocky beds for the winter torrents; cottages placed in the most perilous positions – the day was perfect and cloudless and tho' at so great an elevation it was quite warm – the tints were lovely and the views varying and magnificent – the road was quite dangerous in places and it required a strong nerve to look at the precipice beneath, wh[ere] there were patches of verdure and splendid old trees, with goats and sheep grazing – we crossed the rocks of one torrent – I walked a long way of the dangerous part & then was carried again till we had come to the object of our ride of 10 miles, the Curral, a splendid valley bounded by Mountains wh[ich] come precipitously down to the bottom of fine cliffs of basaltic formation. Craggy Masses also jut up & make distinct ravines; one of these wh[ich] formed the Socorridos ravine is very striking. We clambered a rugged promontory & saw Pico Ruivo, the highest mountain in Madeira, 5000 feet high – the shape of Pico Grande with its natural turrets of rock is however more striking – nr it, looking like a horse's saddle is the Janella where both the Curral & Leira & Agea [Águia] are to be seen – at the bottom to all appearances are a church & village, but they are 500 feet from the bed of the torrent; the cottages looked like beehives, & are surrounded with gardens & vineyards – we then dined on the summit of a lofty ridge & I then sketched having gone considerably down into the ravine & where the road was quite awful, the view amply repaid me.

Driving towards the Curral today you still pass the Church of Santo António, with its twin towers and blue and white striped domes.

Isabella de França stayed at the top and, on 29 November 1853, shows us how her spirits were lifted by the sight:

While we sat here, I thought I saw a butterfly just before me, but instead of a butterfly, it was a large hawk, swooping across the valley to some distant rock; this will give some idea of the diminutiveness of objects seen among these giant peaks. We were now in the clouds; every now and then some romantically formed peak became veiled from our eyes by a light fleecy cloud, which passed over it like a piece of wool; and then the peak stood out again in bold relief against the clear blue sky.

As recently as 1953 Elizabeth Nicholas could write:

The Grand Curral must be visited on a clear day. It is all or nothing. The journey from Funchal takes an hour or less; the road stops abruptly, on the edge of a fantastic cauldron ... At the bottom of this stupendous pit lie clusters of small houses, as distant as a mountain top seen through the wrong end of a telescope.

Then there was still only a mountain path – traces of which remain – down into the cauldron of the Curral das Freiras. But in 1959 a narrow road was constructed winding down to the hamlet where the nuns took refuge in 1566. In the nineteenth century, the nuns rebuilt the sixteenth century chapel.

To visit the Curral das Freiras, you drive 15 miles out of Funchal to Eira do Serrado, a tourist area with the usual facilities. Park and then walk along a path to the lookout. The valley floor is visible 400 metres below, an almost vertical drop, and the mountains rise up in almost circular formation around it. If you are lucky, you may have the lookout to yourself and be able fully to appreciate what you see. Do wear thick soled shoes and take a jacket – the air is fresh and you can become enveloped in cold, clammy cloud from one moment to the next. Indeed, without these accessories in Madeira – at any time of the year – you will be less comfortable.

When you have had your fill of looking, you can drive down into the Curral itself, going back on the approach road a few hundred metres to find the Curral road. The hamlet is now a small town catering a bit for trippers – calling itself a 'mountain resort', with cut-out nuns outside snack bars, and a new, more direct road is being tunnelled through. But don't be put off, many of the inhabitants are still farmers and, further into the Curral, away from the town centre, you can see remnants of life as it has been lived for generations. In spring, it is a mass of blossom, and the views upwards are startling. An up-to-date walking book will advise how to approach on foot which many enthusiasts do.

Catherine of Braganza, Women and Wine

A treaty of friendship had been signed between England and Portugal following the marriage in 1387 of John of Gaunt's daughter **Philippa of Lancaster** (1359–1415) and King João I, giving rise later to the expression 'our oldest ally'. In 1662, Portugal nearly ceded Madeira to England as part of the marriage portion of Catherine of Braganza (1638–1705) when she married Charles II. Although the Queen Regent, **Luisa Maria de Guzman**, originally intended that Madeira form part of her daughter's dowry, it was withdrawn as a stratagem: if England asked for more it would be included. England was satisfied with the dowry first offered but did seek privileges and exemptions in Madeira for its merchants, leading to Britain's later pre-eminent position in the wine trade.

British trade with Madeira was not new: it dated from the middle of the fifteenth century, but now British merchants were settling in numbers on the island, specialising in wine, sugar and property – interests which were to expand over the next two and a half centuries. Emily Smith provides the best description of how the foreign wine merchants were to transform Funchal physically, and a definition of the term *quinta*, when she writes on her arrival in 1841, 'Around the town to the distance of 2 & 3 miles are the innumerable Quintas and Merchants' country seats, with their pleasure grounds and vineyards.'

The British merchants' activities are well-recorded in archives, particularly those of the long-established firm Cossart Gordon. In a 1754 letter book, for example, Elizabeth Nicholas noted a letter of 22

March from merchant Francis Newton (founder of the company): 'Since my arrival here I have been endeavouring to sell your Negro wench but have not yet sold her ...' And she adds that there are many bills of sales relating to 'slaves of various types and nationality' (see also pp. 81–4).

Relations between the British – merchants and consul – and the Portuguese – authorities and merchants – were, from the start, difficult. There are accounts of endless wrangles of one sort or another as they vied with each other commercially. In the midst of at least one such wrangle, we find a Portuguese noblewoman.

Her name was **Dona Guiomar Madalena de Sá Vasconcelos Bettencourt Machado de Vilhena** (1705–1789), known for short as Dona Guiomar de Sá Vilhena and, to me, affectionately rather than disrespectfully, as Guiomar. Her story is told in detail only in Portuguese, I'm afraid, in *Dona Guiomar de Sá Vilhena: Uma Mulher do Século XVIII* (A Woman of the XVIII Century) (2001) by Bernadette Barros.

You do not need me to tell you, her name says it all, that she came from an important and long-established Portuguese-Madeiran family, or number of families. She was the daughter of **Dona Mariana Inés Vilhena** (d.1755) and Francisco Luis Vasconcelos (d. 1717). Her father traded with Brazil, England, North America, the Mediterranean and Portugal, with a fleet of 52 ships. Upon his death, when Guiomar was twelve, her mother, who seems already to have had her own corvette, apparently increased her presence in the business. There is a record of her seeking, in 1751, to export 300 *quintais* of cod, 200 *barricas* of flour, 50 of herrings, 50 of biscuit, and 50 *arrobas* of cheese to Brazil. But her application was rejected by the Judge of the People because of the shortage of provisions in Madeira. The recording of that failure implies that other attempts were successful. On her mother's death in 1755, Guiomar obviously continued those endeavours but there was rather more to her empire than that.

Guiomar was unmarried and had married sisters (and one unmarried) and two brothers, one of whom died in 1723, the other in 1766. She appears to have taken over administration of the interests not only of her own immediate family, such as those of her late father, formally under the trusteeship of her sister **Inácia Maria Rosa de Sá Vilhena's** husband, but also of her extended family dating back generations. The properties under her care included, for example, those of a member of the royal house of France, **Dona Maria de Betencourt**, one of Constança Rodrigues' daughters-in-law (wife of Rui Gonçalves da Câmara, Captain of São Miguel in the Azores, 1473–74) and those of many other women (and men) from whom she and her family, and her family's spouses, were descended.

Many of those properties were chapels founded by women ancestors, but Guiomar's business concerns were also extensive in commodities, particularly sugar and wine. In 1780, for example, she took charge of a sugar plantation in the Ribeira dos Socorridos, apparently the only one which functioned between 1750 and 1782, most of the sugar then being imported from Brazil.

Between 1780 and 1799 (after her death) the house of Dona Guiomar – and her signature DG was stamped on her exports – exported 103,704 pipes of wine, 48,673 of them to Asia. Wine was a means of exchange, in return for imports from Asia of cotton, wool, silk, porcelain, coffee and tea, and from the Americas cereals and timber. In some years, according to customs' records, she was responsible for about 70 per cent of total exports from Madeira. How this marries with Desmond Gregory's suggestion in *The Beneficent Usurpers* (1988) that 'In 1787 ... of eleven thousand pipes of wine that were exported from the island, over six thousand went in British ships and only two thousand in Portuguese', I leave to economic historians to disentangle. It is true that, following her death two years later, and the loss of her exceptional business acumen, confidence and energy, the strength of the empire she left declined.

The governor of Madeira certainly saw DG as one of the two most important commercial houses of Madeira. After he had done her a favour because of this pre-eminence, she penned him a note which has resonances for powerful women throughout the ages:

Neither my gender nor my capabilities are proper for carrying on a profession which depends on many talents; but with Your Excellency's kind protection of all national trade, I have faith in the same kindness as the lights which I consider myself deprived of, which the support of Your Excellency supplies, deigning to be my Protector.

Guiomar not only exported wine, she also produced it – mainly using Malvasia grapes. She bought *fazendas* (farms) in Calheta, Arco da Calheta, and Madalena, Jardim and Paúl do Mar. She had other properties in Funchal, São Roque and Câmara de Lobos (I have only mentioned places that will appear in itineraries). When necessary, she bought ships to transport her wine.

As for the contretemps with the British with which I introduced Guiomar, it was to do with the murder of a British sailor in 1783 during a fracas in which sailors from one of Guiomar's galleys were involved. The British Consul, Charles Murray (1771–99), was acting in British interests but Guiomar, already 78, requisitioned the services of all the notaries in Funchal, leaving Murray no room for manoeuvre.

Guiomar was not only a wily business tycoon and administrator of a vast array of family religious foundations and properties, she was also a collector, especially of fine jewellery, and an admired hostess at her main Funchal residence, Quinta das Angústias. The English diarist William Hickey recorded in 1782 that after

a very good dinner she treated us to several sorts of delicious wine, particularly some malmsey, which she assured us as old as herself, that is seventy years, having been made [by] her father from his own vintages, and precious liquor it undoubtedly was. Claret and Madeira we had plenty of in the same boat so that altogether we made a hearty meal.

Actually, she was 77 then and did not die for another seven years, also at Quinta das Angústias. She was buried in the nearby Angústias cemetery (the site of which is now the Santa Catarina Gardens). We can best meet her physically at that quinta (now Quinta Vigia) in the Funchal Waterfront itinerary (see p. 61).

Guiomar was unusual but not unique as a Portuguese businesswoman in Madeira. Although the received wisdom is that Portuguese upper class women led completely restrained lives, not venturing outside the house without their husbands or, at least, a family member as chaperone, Guiomar's mother was involved in business and Bernadette Barros mentions **Catarina de Mondragão**, wife of Francisco Gonçalves da Câmara and an earlier family member who, in the sixteenth century, owned a ship and a sugar refinery. Widows and mature unmarried women appear to have had different options.

Other than Guiomar's family, I can only find glimpses of women, Portuguese or British, being involved in business. John Foster and his wife were contemporaries of Guiomar, from at least 1757. Then, in the lists of Madeira wineshippers appear entries for the **Widow Foster** & Son (1786–90) and Widow Foster & Co. (1805–09). Any further information has, so far, eluded me. The same is true of **Widow Abudarham** & Sons (fl.1877–1935). But we will meet again **Mrs Durban**, widowed daughter of Thomas Murdoch of Caternach & Murdoch. On his death in 1757, his apprentice John Leacock married Alice Durban, with her 200 guineas, and founded Leacock & Co. During the disastrous vine disease of the 1850s (see also p. 61), the vineyard of Quinta das Maravilhas, owned by the Hon. Caroline Norton, whom you will meet later (see pp. 102–7) was the only one on the island to remain untouched. Whether or not she had anything to do with any aspect of the vineyard is unclear, though it would not be surprising if she did.

Noel Cossart's mother, **Maria Ana Bianchi** (1881–1960), is another exceptional woman about whom there is some record, both written from her son and oral from her grandsons (John Cossart and Anthony Miles). She was tall, strikingly beautiful, strongly independent, ahead of her time and conscious of her background. Her great-grandfather, Giovani de Bianchi – member of a distinguished family from Lake Como, then part of the Austro-Hungarian Empire – came to Madeira in the early nineteenth century. His son, Carlo, married **Ana Perestrelo**

Velosa of the Genoese family which had governed Porto Santo in the fifteenth century. Their son married **Maria Mercedes Lomelino** of the wine family which had come from Genoa in 1470.

Maria Ana Bianchi made a similar wine-oriented alliance when, in 1906, she married Charles Blandy Cossart. By then, she was well initiated into the wine trade. During her childhood, her parents' absences abroad led to happy months spent with her grandfather, Carlo de Bianchi, mostly at his Quinta Cristovão at Machico. So close did they become that he adopted her; when her engagement was announced in the English papers, she had both natural parents and an adopted one.

Carlo's son, Maria's father, was the godson of Maximilian of Austria which meant that, when royal visitors came to Madeira, Carlo had social responsibilities and, as a widower, he required a hostess. Young Maria played the part. The result of this upbringing with her grandfather led her son to write later: 'She learnt a great deal about wine, acquired his magnificent palate and after she married my father she directed all the blending at Cossarts. She was also a partner in Lomelino with her two brothers.'

She was also an excellent cook – herself producing a banquet when the Empress Elizabeth of Austria came to dine. Before it was commonplace, she camped on the Desertas Islands and, before the First World War, when the first pilots to cross the Atlantic from Portugal to Brazil (Gago Coutinho and Sacadura Cabral) passed through Madeira, it was Maria Bianchi Cossart who went for a spin in their seaplane.

Widowed young, she did not remarry but had a long-standing relationship – keeping separate establishments – with the wine trader João de Belen of Câmara de Lobos who, when he died, left his firm partly to members of her family who had worked with him.

More recently, in 1972, **Dona Manuela de Freitas**, daughter of Mario Barbeito, began to help her father with running the family's business. She helped build up the export side and, in 1980, more or less took charge of the Barbeito company; after her father's death in 1985 she ran it single-handedly until she retired in 1992.

A hundred and fifty years after Dona Guiomar, Edith Hutcheon gives a lovely flavour of Madeira's eponymous wine in a chapter on the subject in *Things Seen in Madeira* (1928):

Like the rest of the world, I fell a victim to an influenza epidemic, once upon a time in Funchal, and an autocratic doctor prescribed a glass of Madeira twice a day. I objected. I never drank wine. I disliked wine. Wine never agreed with me. I might have saved my breath. He paused until I had finished, and then continued as though I had not spoken: 'You will take two glasses of Madeira a day, one at lunch and one at dinner. You may trust the wines at ——' And lo! from the heavens dropped, or from a mysterious cellar rose, a magic bottle with the date 1864 – precious sixty-year-old bottled liquid sunshine – rich, soft, and of a mellowness! sent to me by a friend long resident in Madeira. Naturally after this I was fastidious about my wine.

Anglo-Saxon Influences

In spite of the economic success of British wine merchants, Protestant inhabitants of Madeira were not permitted to be buried there; indeed, should Protestant burials be discovered, the corpses were dug up and thrown into the sea. In 1765, however, pressure ensured that finally a cemetery for non-Roman Catholics was secured. An English church was built in 1822.

In the nineteenth century, the Protestant cemetery became the final resting place for foreigners with consumption, particularly British, seeking a cure in the salubrious dry, warm, winter air of Madeira. In fact the healing climate is a bit of a myth: Madeira can be rather humid and, at Monte, where sanatoriums were built, it can be positively cold and damp – though half-way up the hill is a little better. There is a theory that Madeira's reputation was fostered so that it could act as a quarantine outpost for those returning to Britain from the East, particularly India.

So much a part of the Funchal scene did these visitors become that Lady Emmeline Stuart-Wortley, who wrote for effect and did not care much for the Madeira she visited in 1851, complained:

Many a pallid, ghastly face, have I seen at Madeira, projecting itself from the half-drawn curtains of palanquins, many an altered, haggard countenance, which gave one the sad idea, that after a few airings, the sufferer would exchange the palanquin for the coffin ...

And even the usually sanguine **Marianne North** (1830–1890), the renowned traveller-botanist-artist, seemed to gain only one firm impression of Madeira when her ship stopped there for a few days in January 1875; she wrote:

I had a cousin there with a sick husband, and in spite of the marvellous beauty of the surroundings I pitied her for having such a number of hopeless invalids all round her. I heard coughs and groans on every side, and saw poor bloodless faces carried about in hammocks on men's shoulders covered with white drapery, and looking like corpses.

Edith Hutcheon, writing in 1928, quotes Marianne and then castigates her:

So much for the impression of a passing traveller; far other is the picture given by those resident in the Island, who speak of the wonderful gaiety and spirits of the invalids, the garden parties and the riding parties, the too great exertions and recklessness which often led to sad relapses. It was far from being the despairing hospital or *Frieden[s]heim* [home of peace] of Miss North.

You will meet some named invalids later (pp. 74–80) to judge how they fit these images. **Queen Adelaide** (1792–1849), widow of William IV of England, spent several months in Madeira for her health in the winter of 1847–48, staying at Quinta das Angústias. During her visit she gave generously to the poor, even building, according to her biographer, a new road from the Ribeiro Seco (now under the bridge between Reid's and the Savoy hotels) to Câmara de Lobos for the fisherfolk. Isabella de França suggests, however, that the amount required was so large that, in the end, Queen Adelaide made only a substantial contribution.

Madeira didn't do the Queen's health much good, nor did the road lastingly benefit the inhabitants of Câmara de Lobos though in its day it was the only bit of flat road there was (see p. 66).

During the Napoleonic Wars, from 1807 to 1814, the British flag was raised in Madeira, and British troops were stationed there, which apparently accounts for many inhabitants of Anglo-Saxon appearance round the former garrison towns of Santo da Serra and Camacha. This is not an uncommon Madeiran explanation: the same is said of British Consul Henry Veitch, in Madeira a little later. He was alleged to have had mistresses in several villages, leaving behind generations of fair-haired children. He would, it is said, hoist the British flag when his wife, **Caroline T. Veitch**, was in residence, and the Portuguese when she was not; she nevertheless erected a mausoleum 'as a tribute to his memory' when he was buried in their garden at Quinta do Jardim da Serra. There is a limited connection between Veitch's escapades and Madeira's reputation in some quarters as 'the island of British bastards'. Before the 1960s, it was apparently where unmarried women went from Britain to have 'unwanted' babies.

Those British who became part of a flourishing mercantile community after Catherine of Braganza's marriage created for themselves a privileged way of life and were often unpopular with the Portuguese, partly because it was suspected that Britain had its territorial eye on Madeira. Emily Shore, a well-educated and thoughtful 19-year-old Englishwoman who came to Madeira suffering from consumption in December 1838, confided her firm opinion on the matter to her diary, published as *The Journal of Emily Shore* (1898; 1991):

Miss Telles came this morning and gave us another lesson in Portuguese ... She told us a great deal about the English residents in Madeira, who, she says, have most of them risen from the condition of small clerks and shopkeepers; ... and then, having very quickly made their money, they packed off their children, says Miss T., to be educated in England. These now assume great airs, look down on the Portuguese, and will not associate with them, which, she says, once made her think they must be the finest people in the world, but, when she came to England, she soon found the absurdity of their pretensions ...

All the residents speak an infamously bad Portuguese, as is natural, if they will not condescend to associate with the Portuguese gentry.

Miss Teles, if I am not mistaken, came from a noble family. Fanny Anne Burney Wood (a great niece of the novelist and diarist) was there at the same time for the health of Jane Wood, her husband's niece; she approached the matter rather differently:

Some of the higher classes of Portuguese are generally invited by Residents to their Evening parties, but on the whole there is not much intercourse between the natives and the English, which is unfortunate, as a contrary system would probably create a pleasanter feeling towards us generally than at present exists among the Madeirans, who are extremely jealous of our superiority. A little civility occasionally costs people nothing, and is much valued by the Portuguese, who are themselves scrupulously polite and obliging.

She goes on to add, in that diary entry of 7 May 1839, with the same lack of awareness that existed until recently in her own country about its practices, 'The Portuguese, though very polite to the fair sex generally, make no scruple about beating their wives ...'

In spite of their economic power, the number of snooty British people was not great: in 1819, for example, there were only 100, 'including women, children, clerks and servants'. Twenty years later, it was 500, swollen to 700 in the winter. (Madeira's population was 120,000 of which 30,000 lived in Funchal.)

It was only in the last quarter of the twentieth century, I am reliably told, that social barriers between the two communities began to be dismantled. Now, relations are completely relaxed, particularly among the young. Differences between historical interpretations are inevitable and these have had a tendency to increase rather than otherwise as indigenous historians have gained confidence in Madeira as a place in its own right.

What the Portuguese Roman Catholics made of the English Protestants during an internecine row which came to a head in 1847, is mostly left to the imagination. Even Dowager Queen Adelaide inadvertently played a fringe role, as did a relative of Miss Teles, the Portuguese teacher. The palaver had two strands which seem to have gone their separate ways. The first concerned the Reverend R.T. Lowe and that is discussed in intricate detail in *Scandal in Madeira* (Roy Nash, 1990) – a book very difficult to come by. The second strand was the activities of Dr Robert Kalley which are described in some detail in the more available *The Beneficent Usurpers.*

From 1833, Richard Lowe was pastor at the English Church in Funchal. His name today is better known as a naturalist but for many years among the British colony in Madeira it was synonymous for some with 'Romish tendencies'; he leaned towards the newly burgeoning Oxford Movement. Emily Shore, whose father was a parson but whose opinions were her own, pronounced in her diary on 17 March 1839: 'Mr ——'s two sermons were intensely high church and Puseyite; the most intolerable notions delivered dogmatically and positively, without any attempt at reasoning or argument.' For others, he was a learned and principled champion. Dr Kalley was a fiery Scots Calvinist who arrived in Madeira in 1838 and started proselytising among his Portuguese patients and the British community.

The only glimpse of a link I have found is provided in the unpublished diary of Emily Smith, an obviously devout woman who arrived in Madeira with her family in 1841. Lowe's sermons made her increasingly agitated. She wrote, for example, on 14 November 1841, 'At Church heard more painful and unscriptured things from Mr Lowe ... the Lord keep us from such heresies.' Dr Kalley, who held weekly prayer meetings in his drawing room, was, however, completely to her taste; she wrote on 19 November of 'Good Dr Kalley who is such a witness for the Truth among the poor Portuguese.' But that year the Roman Catholic Governor of Madeira warned Kalley to stop his proselytising. Kalley recorded that Portuguese women who attended his meetings were accused of being prostitutes. He pulled back but, after a period of leave in Scotland, he returned, keener than ever. He was arrested in 1843. A petition was sent to the British Foreign Office on his behalf signed by eminent supporters on the island who included the new **Duchess of Manchester** (née Millicent Sparrow, d. 1848, wife of the 6th Duke).

Meanwhile, Lowe had also gone on home leave and returned with a wife, **Catherine Maria Guerin** (1802–1874). She found herself ostracised by half the British colony; indeed it became split, with whole families refusing to speak to former friends and neighbours.

In 1846, a new Portuguese Governor, who believed the British were trying to buy up the island, was appointed. Kalley was back practising and proselytising which resulted in his converts being punished – one a woman who was sentenced to death for blasphemy and heresy, a sentence commuted to five years' imprisonment. Matters came to a head later that year when Father Congego Teles apparently incited the local populace to attack one of Kalley's 60-strong prayer meetings in the home of the **Misses Rutherford**. The police did nothing to protect those being beaten up, nor the two women. Emily Smith had described the nieces of Lord Sinclair in 1841: 'the youngest is very delicate, just recovering from the scarletina; her bronchia and chest are diseased – her sister is an excellent pleasing person'. They were probably **Anne** (born 1815) and **Margaret** (born 1816), daughters of the wine merchant James Rutherford and his wife **Mary Buckley**.

A week later, following a similar incident, Kalley escaped to a British ship in the bay disguised as a sick woman, together with the Misses Rutherford. What became of **Mrs Kalley** who, on 21 December 1841, Emily Smith had noted 'coughed much and seemed very poorly', and her mother **Mrs Crawford** is unclear.

But the members of the British community attending the English Church seem to have been too torn apart over Richard Lowe to notice Kalley. By this time, the Bishop of London and Lord Palmerston, the Foreign Secretary, were at each other's throats over the matter;

Queen Victoria had been sent three testimonials – one against Lowe and two for (including one from himself). Of his 75 supporters, 30 were women. Those against Lowe on the committee of the Church stopped his salary and that of the organist, **Miss Ellen Hayward**. When **Miss Mary Phelps** (1822–1893) turned up to play the organ, unpaid, she found herself enmeshed in this unholy row: Mr (William Burton) Penfold, treasurer, and Mr (Charles Ridpath) Blandy, trustee, 'respectfully request Miss Phelps will have the kindness to state by whose authority she acted on that occasion' (January 1847).

The Phelps family and Lowe were friends of long standing: Mary's unpublished diary, kept between 1839 and 1843 – not, unfortunately, including these events – records countless visits between them, and Mary and Lowe often played in recitals together. But she, as perhaps opposed to other members of her family, did not necessarily approve of his leanings, nor indeed of his sermons, which she often described as 'unintelligible'. She went further on 23 May 1840:

... when Mr Lowe took me into another room to look at shells I began talking about and abusing him, for which he of course scolded and lectured me, saying that his interpretations of Scriptures were the real ones and ours the fanciful, but still I was unconvinced, as I am by almost all his arguments. Indeed he is so violent and goes, I am sure, so much too far in his exclusiveness, that he is more in danger of so disgusting me as to make me Low Church instead of higher than I am, which I think is high enough in all conscience. And yet how can one be disgusted with anything Mr Lowe says or does.

Her last sentence seems to explain the loyalty of the family whose members, including 18-year-old Mary, and even twelve-year-old Harriett, signed the testimonial. I note, though, that there is only one Elizabeth Phelps and both mother, descended from Huguenots, and eldest daughter, had that name. (Miss Phelps, Bella, will play her own part later in Madeira's history, see pp. 28–32.)

The wrangling continued. At a meeting set up to try and resolve matters, unbecoming language was used – 'four ladies present'. At the end of 1847, Queen Adelaide, not realising what was going on, attended Lowe's services and even had him and his wife to dine. She did, however, then remember that she had brought her own chaplain; she would not 'enter into the squabbles of the place'.

A new vicar was appointed by Palmerston and refused a licence from the Bishop of London whose toes the Foreign Secretary had trodden on. So Lowe set up his own church, commandeering the silver plate from his erstwhile church, in Rua das Aranhas, known as the Becco. By 1850, the Becco had a congregation of 140.

Eventually, in 1852, it seems that Catherine Maria Lowe – whom many women had, for nearly ten years, apparently crossed the road to avoid – put her foot down. Through family connections, she obtained her husband a new living in England and they departed. Many of Lowe's supporters returned to the English Church – and there was a memorable scene on the Sunday they did so – but the rump of the Becco Church did not give in until 1893; in earlier years that included the Phelps family who, however, left Madeira in the early 1860s. The building was apparently demolished in 1985 but, although the site is said now to be a traffic island, I cannot find a convincing one; indeed, I am satisfied that a 1930s description (Newall) of an 'old Spanish mansion' with the date 1606 over a 'square gateway' and lying within a 'picturesque courtyard of triangular shape' is of a building that survives, though modernised, just up on the right when approaching Rua das Aranhas from Avenida Arriaga.

The Lowes returned to Madeira several times in the years to come, partly to encourage the Becco congregation, but mostly for Lowe's work as a naturalist (and we will meet his women collaborators later, see pp. 102–7). In 1874, when the Lowes were once more on their way to Madeira, the SS *Liberia* went missing, its fate never to be established. A memorial was erected to the turbulent priest and his long-suffering wife in the Protestant Cemetery.

How much lasting hurt had been caused to the British community by the battle royal can only be speculated upon. Isabella de França mentions the 'schism' in her diary of 1853, but later visitors do not.

Women caught up in the row, such as the Penfolds, appear in happier days in 'Flowers, Gardens and Walks' (see pp. 129–31).

Queen Maria II da Gloria (1819–1853)

Following the upheavals of the Napoleonic Wars which ended in 1815, unsettled times came again to Madeira between 1821 and 1834. A simplified history lesson is necessary: João VI of Portugal, Regent for his insane mother until 1816 and king thereafter, was forced by Napoleon to flee to the Portuguese colony of Brazil in 1807, and remained there until 1822 when Brazil declared its independence. As the new country was prepared to have a monarch, the Brazilian throne was given to João's elder son, Pedro, known as Emperor Pedro I of Brazil. There he married **Leopoldina of Austria** (1797–1826) who, in 1817, went out to Rio to marry him via Madeira (see p. 159). They had a daughter, Maria da Gloria in 1819. In 1820, there was a revolution in Portugal and when King João returned there in 1822 he was obliged to rule as a constitutional monarch until he died in 1826, leaving the throne to his son Pedro. Pedro, however, was unwilling to leave his Brazilian throne so, instituting a parliamentary charter in Portugal, he decreed that his seven-year old daughter Maria should rule there in his stead, with his brother Dom Miguel as Regent. After two years Dom Miguel, who was also Maria's betrothed, overthrew her and took complete power for himself. In Madeira, his followers (Miguelites) rounded up anyone they considered loyal to the Portuguese Constitution and the Queen (Pedrists).

Emily Shore, during her five-month stay in 1838–39, describes the part played by the foreign community, as told to her by an Englishman also in Madeira to regain his health:

He told us that the English merchants here are popular or unpopular according as they acted during the war of Pedro and Miguel, when Miguel's party possessed the island; for the English, being unmolested, were not obliged to take either side, and as their houses were never searched, they were able to conceal in their stores and cellars persecuted individuals of the Pedroite party. This many of them did very generously, as Mr Phelps, Mr Wallace [Wallas], and some others. But Mr ——— (such, at least, is the story) voluntarily gave up his best clerk, who had served him faithfully for many years, to the Miguelites. If this is really true, Mr ——— acted basely, and deserves the dislike with which he is regarded by the Portuguese.

Fanny Burney Wood, with access to similar informants, caps that story:

During the struggle between Dom Miguel and his niece, the followers of the former were most violent. Many families were obliged to quit the island on account of their political principles. An order was published warning the English residents not to appear in the streets after eight o'clock at night. The Consul also ordered that no English persons should wear Dona Maria's colours, of blue and white, in the streets for fear of being insulted by the Miguelites. Three English ladies chose purposely to brave public opinion and feeling, and walked out the next day in the noxious colours; in consequence they were driven home by the soldiers and desired to remove the obnoxious badges.

Their identity is yet to be discovered. The English visitor in 1853–54, Isabella de França, had more entrée to the local community than usual because her husband was not only of Madeiran extraction but still had lands and position there. She recounts what had happened to two members of the clergy in the vicinity of her husband's lands just inland from the west coast during the Miguelite period:

On our return we met the Vicar of the Estreito [da Calheta], a very gentlemanly man, who had suffered a great deal in the Miguelite times, having been in prison here and in Lisbon all through the reign of Miguel. He was then Curate of the same parish. His predecessor who was then Vicar, was also a most respectable man, and suffered still more, being old and infirm, and consequently not so well able to bear the miseries of a prison. They were both marked men from the first beginning of the troubles, for when the first Constitution fell, in 1823, and Judges were sent out with a Commission to try the Constitutionalists, the greatest efforts were made to implicate them. Any evidence against them was eagerly received. One old woman actually swore that she had seen the Vicar going to a meeting of Freemasons, on the back of his Satanic Majesty, and this was received, and recorded as evidence ...

Sarah Bowdich, who left Madeira on 26 October 1823, just after the trouble started, confirmed Isabella's contention when she wrote, 'Depositions were taken, without searching into the character of witnesses; false oaths seemed trifles, when old women or young boys had any spite to gratify.'

William Henry Koebel, whose work on Madeira fills one or two gaps, paraphrases at some length the letters of a **Miss Chalmers** without saying where he saw them or further identifying her. She provided an eyewitness account of the Miguelite takeover and of the rescue of the mainly British refugees – including herself, the ousted Portuguese Governor and his family – from Funchal by the British frigate *Alligator*.

As a result of all this, Queen Maria's father abdicated in 1831 from his Brazilian throne and, arriving in England with his daughter, called on the British and French Governments to help regain her Portuguese throne. This they did and in Madeira, where people had been much-buffeted politically for more than ten years, 'Every window and balcony throughout the days was filled with ladies all dressed in constitutional colours, waving without intermission their white handkerchiefs and singing patriotic airs ...', wrote the partisan British Consul. Maria reigned again between 1834 and 1853 when she died in childbirth aged only 34.

Life had returned to normal in Madeira but, on receipt of the news of the Queen's death, it was briefly disrupted again, as Isabella de França writes with feeling:

... at ten o'clock in the morning, a heavy gun was fired from the Peak Fort, almost over our heads, and answered by one from the Ilheo [Loo] on the other side of us. The noise made by the gun from the Peak, shook every window in the house; that from the Ilheo being a little farther off, was less stunning, but the echoes of the two reverberated from mountain to mountain, like not very distant thunder. These guns continued to fire every five minutes, for three days, and two nights, so that it was utterly impossible to get a moment's rest, either by day or night. The report was so loud, that however you might prepare yourself for it, it was impossible to avoid jumping the moment you heard it; it was in vain that I tried to keep the windows tolerably still by forcing wedges into them; the moment the gun fired down went the wedges, and everything jumped whether animate or inanimate. The night brought no relief, as I lay with my head under the bed clothes, the merciless guns still fired heavily, & shook me in my bed; the morning came, and then the night came, and then the morning came again, and still the heavy reports continued without intermission at every five minutes, night and day. ...

At last, for the sake of the invalids at least, the Governor was prevailed upon to stop the noise, at sunset on the third day.

Princess Maria Amélia (1831–1853)

Relations between Brazil and Madeira were always close; often migrants from Portugal to Brazil, or vice versa, stopped on their way in Funchal; migrants from both places settled in Madeira. The significance of these ties was made flesh and blood for me by an email from a Brazilian friend whose family I knew had some Madeiran origins. She told me the story of her Aunt Lourdes who had been, as she put it, an 'angry' girl. One of Lourdes' grandparents had been born in Madeira, another in Portugal. Then, as Nancy Ferraz explained Lourdes' behaviour in Brazil:

Lourdes had two cousins. When the three girls were playing, Lourdes was the leader, bossy and demanding obedience. If the others didn't obey, Lourdes would start fighting, making her cousins cry. She never cried. The cousins went to their Portuguese grandmother to complain. She replied, 'Don't cry, and don't worry. Lourdes is *ilhoa*' (an islander – because her other parent was from Madeira). This had a particular meaning in my family – that an *ilhoa* has a strong, dominating personality. And this idea was not only part of my childhood but has remained with me – that both strands of my ancestry taught me the need for determination to succeed, particularly the Madeiran.

There is more concrete evidence of those ties. In 1852, **Dona Amélia** (née de Leuchtenberg), **Dowager Empress of Brazil** (1792–1876) arrived in Funchal to stay at Quinta das Angústias. She had been the second wife (1829) of Maria da Gloria's father, Pedro I. She was bringing her daughter, Dona Maria Amélia, in the hope that the salubrious air would cure her tuberculosis. It was ineffectual and Maria Amélia died, aged 21. The following year, to commemorate her life, her mother founded the Hospício (sanatorium) for the consumptive poor, the building of which, opposite the Quinta das Angústias, was completed in 1862, with the Empress' sister, Queen Josephine of Sweden, as trustee. And, in 1880, an orphanage was erected alongside, both establishments run by nuns of the Order of St Vincent de Paul (see pp. 62–3).

Bella Phelps and Embroidery

The 1850s were a particularly grim time for Madeira. In 1856, for example, between 7,000 and 10,000 died from cholera in a few weeks. As if that was not enough, devastation had begun to come from another quarter in 1852 and reached its apogee in 1853: vineyards from which Madeira's main export was produced were afflicted with *oïdium tuckeri*, a fast-spreading leaf mould which inhibits the formation of grapes – an attack which lasted for ten or so years. Households in the countryside were in danger of destitution. Into this vacuum stepped 33-year-old Miss Phelps (1820–1893).

Bella Phelps was the eldest of seven daughters (and four sons) of the Anglo-Madeiran scholar and wine producer Joseph Phelps and **Elizabeth Dickinson** whom he had married in 1819. We have already met one of their daughters, Mary, as diarist and organist at the English Church. The family was not only numerous but its members have been described as physically large. This included Bella about whom it was recorded that she 'was found with [the hip] bath firmly fixed round her like the shell of a snail, and she was only liberated by the concentrated action of the entire family'. I am not convinced by this caricature of the family. Mary Phelps' diary

– mainly full of social to-ings and fro-ings and the heartsearchings, affections and jealousies of a girl entering womanhood – is full of self-analysis and never suggests anxiety about her size, or that of her siblings, whose amours, including physical descriptions of partners, she also records. Her sister **Fanny** (1826–1890) was described, when she became stepmother of the archaeologist Sir Arthur Evans in 1859, as 'rather small and a little plump' (not gross). Whatever their size, it was no bar to Bella's action.

It had not taken her mother long to start a girls' school (with a Mrs Blackburn), similar to one for boys set up by her husband, nor to notice that the lack of trees (following the years of tree burning in the fifteenth century) was a block to Madeira's well-being. Elizabeth Dickinson Phelps initiated and organised a reforestation project, sending to England for seeds and saplings and getting them planted, often by guests on picnics. It was not surprising, therefore, that Bella should act similarly at the first sign of need.

When at times the British have been unpopular in Madeira, the part they have played in its development has been minimised, but **Elizabeth Nicholas**, a *Sunday Times* travel journalist who visited Madeira four times between 1951 and 1953 for her book *A Traveller's Notebook,* explored the positive claims made about Bella Phelps and found them borne out by the facts. (Unfortunately, Mary Phelps' diary stops long before these events).

Bella had done charity work at an orphanage in Santana (just to the north-west of Funchal and not to be confused with the better-known town) run by nuns and there helped teach the children to embroider. Embroidery was already an occupation of Portuguese noblewomen, particularly those confined to convents such as the Santa Clara. Weaving had been introduced from Holland with the second batch of settlers and Bella noticed that the country women of Madeira were also nimble-fingered so, when hard times hit, she set up an embroidery school apparently on the family estate using her own designs.

3. Bella Phelps' embroidery design, from Cossart, *The Island Vineyard*

Where this estate was, I have been unable to determine. In the 1830s and 1840s, the family's country place was Quinta Prazer ('Pleasure') on Monte, just below where the Tropical Gardens are now but that quinta was sold in 1847 (see also pp. 147–9).

Bella was joined by Miss Selby and Mrs Hope who taught lace-making. But it was the embroidery that took off, by 1858 employing 1,000 women and filling a hole in the economy. At first the embroidery was sold privately but, by the time the Phelps family left Madeira in the early 1860s, Bella had found agents in London to continue the work of export, and they established themselves in Madeira. The industry continued to expand until now it is an important part of Madeira's prosperity. Some 20,000 islanders are involved in the industry, at least one fifth of the working population. Today the visitor who wishes to bring away some memento from Madeira will undoubtedly choose embroidery, from a baby's robe to the most intricately beautiful (if slightly impractical) table linen, each piece having attached to it the lead seal of approval of the IBTAM Handicrafts Industry. (See details of their museum in the itinerary on p. 111.)

From the beginning it was a cottage industry, and it still is. While the planning, designing, pricking out of the design, finishing and administration are done in factories in Funchal (which can also be visited to watch the processes), the embroidery is done by women – *bordadeiras* – in their homes. (At periods of peak demand, the men of the family have been known to apply their fingers). As Elizabeth Nicholas wrote in 1953:

Anyone who drives out of Funchal on an afternoon excursion is bound to be struck by the groups seated round the cottage doorsteps; the women involved are tough, resilient country women, but their work is of exquisite fineness, on the most delicate fabrics. The virtuosity they display seems incongruous; one does not, somehow, expect a woman whose hands are toughened by the hard labours of peasant husbandry to handle a needle as delicate as any employed by a Parisian *haute couturière*. Yet so it is; and it is interesting to speculate on this strange and very wonderful facility the Madeirense has for all delicate work.

In spite of this emphasis on home industry, a 1924 account (Alan Lethbridge) tells of visiting a 'factory' where 400 women worked – in conditions that were airy and comfortable. Some of them had their babies with them, and 'children' of 'tender years' also worked on more simple designs. By that time, the industry employed as many as 7,000 people.

There is some evidence of trade union activity among the embroiderers as early as 1856. Over a century later, in 1976, following the revolution in Portugal of 1974, homeworkers really began to build their own union; indeed, Madeira can be said to have been in advance of similar unions being set up in the rest of the world. Their first substantial success was to obtain the right to be covered by social security – pension rights and child and sickness benefits. Nearly 4,000 home embroiderers were unionised and active by the 1980s; there are now about 8,000 members.

Having received no reply to a letter to the Union headquarters seeking information, I established by telephone that no one there spoke English. This was confirmed when I visited the premises – which include several unions – at 151–2 Rua dos Ferreiros. I was, nevertheless, greeted warmly by a group of women embroidering there under the Union banner – a moving experience for anyone interested in women's concerns. I got the Union information I give here from the internet.

The deftness and patience that enabled countrywomen to embroider so beautifully ironically also meant they were called on when treatment against *oïdium tuckeri* was eventually developed. It was they who wielded the bellows and brushes applying sulphur to the vines at the season when the skins of the grapes began to shine. At harvest time, barefooted, in light gowns and white linen jackets, and with red and yellow kerchiefs, they did their share of picking the grapes too; but they were paid less than the men. Families again had to depend on the income from embroidery when another vine disease, *phylloxera vastatrix* – which attacked the roots – hit the wine industry in the 1870s.

What Bella Phelps would have made of developments we can only guess. There is still a Largo do Phelps at the end of the Rua do Carmo where the Phelps had a house and the firm its stores beneath – a common tradition, apparently to protect families from marauders. At least one guide book says that it was named after Bella – I hope so.

Almost a hundred years after Bella Phelps left Madeira, you might have been surprised to see a Phelps embroidery shop in the centre of Funchal. It was set up in 1952 by **Greta Monica Phelps**, a great-niece of Bella's, who came to Madeira, seized her opportunity and, in 1960, married into another established Madeiran embroidery business.

Women's Places

From Funchal Eastwards

Lazareto, Santa Cruz, Lazareto continued, Machico, Santo da Serra, Camacha

Part of Madeira's continuing history, tied to its places, its women (inhabitants and visitors) and the books they wrote, is best told in a journey by road from Funchal to Machico and back.

Lazareto

As you leave Funchal, ignore the signs to the airport; instead, take the coast road which is still quite unspoilt and now, because of the diversion of the main stream of traffic, allows you to dawdle and enjoy the coastal scenery – the sea sparkling below to your right, the neat gardens and rising hills to your left. But keep your eyes skinned for a ravine ahead cutting from inland to the sea, with a large barrack-like building on the edge; here was the Lazareto ('House of St Lazarus'), also known as the Fever Hospital of Gonçalves Aires.

Lady Emmeline Stuart-Wortley (1806–1855), daughter of the Duke of Rutland, who visited Madeira briefly in 1851 as a side trip from Portugal, gave a useful introduction as she steamed towards Funchal and noted that 'The new quarantine establishment is, I understand, situated at the entrance of a bold mountain gorge that diversifies the scenery here.' Once she arrived, she was her usual unrestrained self – she made money from her travel writing and keeping it nicely provocative. Indeed, the English bookseller in Funchal today, where you can find the odd secondhand book as well as new ones about Madeira, is apt to dismiss her and her book – *A Visit to Portugal and Madeira* (1854) – suggesting that she is much resented by islanders. He almost implies that he would not stock it even if he could come by a copy. It can be found on the internet but too highly priced for me. She wrote:

Notwithstanding the beauty of this charming climate, the inhabitants of the island suffer from some horrible diseases; for instance from elephantiasis and lepra: The São Lazaro hospital is said to contain numerous cases of these hideous disorders. This is supposed to be mainly owing to the paucity of wholesome food, indeed, of any food among the poor here, and also to the injurious inattention of the peasantry to cleanliness. These circumstances are mischievously operated on by the warmth of the temperature. It is sad to think of such loathsome horrors amidst scenes so lovely as these.

Ellen Taylor, following her 1880–81 visit, wrote, 'The Leper Hospital at São Lazaro was built by the town council in 1665. The few lepers there are chiefly from the Western districts of the island.' She seems to be referring to the original quarantine hospital near the Santa Catarina Chapel in the centre of town, if you read both her editions carefully; but mention of the chapel is left out of the second edition, suggesting the correction of a mistake. Certainly there was such an establishment earlier because a British doctor (Joseph Adams) visiting it in 1803 noted that there were ten women there, with a midwife available. From a list he had access to, starting in 1702, there were no women mentioned until 1746, when there were 20. There is also an 1842 watercolour painted from the Lazareto in town (see p. 60) showing that the building, at least, was still in place. By Ellen Taylor's day, however, if we follow Lady Emmeline's 1851 and subsequent accounts, the working institution had been moved out of town to the gorge east of Funchal.

In 1819, in spite of the Lazareto, there were apparently still lepers on the loose in Funchal – a scandal according to one anonymous commentator because it allowed them 'to traverse the streets, to the peril of those ladies who are in "the way that ladies wish to be, who love their lords"'. The Lazareto may or may not have been used for lepers; it was certainly used to quarantine suspect visitors.

The most evocative description of the Lazareto – one which even today is not entirely out of place – comes from Isabella de França in 1853. She often went about on horseback but it was of her first ride in a palanquin (a conveyance on a pole shouldered by two men) that she wrote (and painted):

We descended by some terrible Voltas, or zigzags to a bridge across the ravine at the mouth of which on the sea stands the Lazaretto. It is a wild romantic looking spot. The sides of the ravine are formed of black volcanic rocks, still shewing evident marks of having been deposited in a semi-fluid state. In some places they overhang one another, in others they rise in a succession of gigantic steps, and wherever a foot or two of something not nearer the perpendicular than forty five degrees could be found, or made by terracing the walls of black stone, there is an attempt at cultivation; either a vine, a fig, or a peach tree, half a dozen stalks of wheat, some sweet potatoes, or all these together, as they can find room. Where the rocks are too bare for cultivation they are covered with prickly pear, brambles, and the yellow coronella, now in flower. Down one side and up the other, winds the high road to Sta Cruz and Machico ... the buildings consist of two dwelling rooms, and a kitchen ... At the back is a long terrace walk, through what was once a vineyard, leading to the gate, which opens at the foot of the bridge and is guarded by a sentry. Here the inmates converse over the wall with their friends standing on the bridge. On the other side of the river is a fountain, frequented by washerwomen, and a guard house, where a serjeant's guard is stationed, whenever the Lazaretto is occupied. At the time we were there, an American Officer was performing quarantine, and he said he was very comfortable; as long as there were not more than six or eight inmates, it was not a bad place to be in.

The Lazareto will have increased significance when we have met Mary Jane Wilson in Santa Cruz.

4. Isabella de França approaching the Lazareto, 1853, courtesy of Frederico de Freitas Museum

Santa Cruz

Our first historical description of Santa Cruz comes from Emily Shore in December 1838 as she approached the island where she hoped to recover:

... The sun had not yet risen, but I could see from my little window that we were sailing past the noble coast of Madeira, and that the little white town of Santa Cruz was visible ... The morn had risen in glowing beauty, and through an atmosphere that no English summer can equal, we looked on the magnificent pile of rugged mountains that rose abruptly out of the deep ocean, and pierced the clouds with their summits.

Emily Smith provides a closer view of Santa Cruz when, in 1842, she visited the Blandy Quinta, Reveredo, and sketched from it. (The quinta – next to the new library near the chapel – now belongs to Santa Cruz Council and, with its large garden and amphitheatre built onto the side, is used for functions and exhibitions.)

5. Santa Cruz from Quinta Reveredo, by Emily Smith, 1842, courtesy of Quinta das Cruzes Museum

A feel of Santa Cruz in the 1920s visited by sea comes from the pen of Edith Hutcheon:

From any of the villages on the east coast one may return to Funchal, if so minded, by launch or the local daily steamer, and more and more one grows to love this near view of the glorious coast, of which perhaps Santa Cruz, a little town at the mouth of a great ravine, is the gem. Most picturesque are its colour-washed houses and lofty mountain guardians as viewed from the sea.

In July 1875, **Lady (Annie) Brassey** (1839–1887) and her family approached Funchal in the yacht in which they travelled the world, and she noted in *A Voyage in the 'Sunbeam'* (1878):

As we rapidly approached the land, the beauty of the scenery became more fully apparent. We steamed slowly along the east coast, passing many pretty hamlets, nestled in bays or perched on the side of the hills, and observing how every possible nook and corner seemed to be terraced and cultivated. Nearly all the cottages in the island are inhabited by a simple people, many of whom have never left their native villages, even to look at the magnificent view from the top of the surrounding mountains, or to gaze on the sea, by which they are encompassed.

THE 'SUNBEAM'

6.   The Brasseys' yacht from Brassey, *A Voyage in the 'Sunbeam'*

Katherine Routledge (1866–1935), who was to describe Easter Island in a way never surpassed, recorded much the same observation in *The Mystery of Easter Island*, as they stopped for a few hours in Madeira on their year-long journey to the Pacific on the yacht *Mana* in 1914. And she added in Funchal,

We regretted that we were unable to stay longer and see something of the life in those lonely cottages among the mountains which we had seen from the sea, where the women are said to add considerably to their income by the embroidery for which the island is famous.

At the time of my final writing you can go to Machico from Funchal and back by boat, but not stopping at Santa Cruz, and only on a Tuesday (10.30a.m. to 1.00p.m.); I missed the chance – ask at the Marina on the waterfront for up-to-date information (see p. 58).

When you reach Santa Cruz, still little more than a village, ask someone the way to Rua Irmã (Sister) Wilson – they are bound to know. **Mary Jane Wilson** (1840–1916) arrived in Madeira in 1881. She had been born in India but her mother (née Mary James) died when she was eight months old. Her father (Captain Charles Wilson of the Indian Army) did what he could but, when Mary Jane was three, he sent her and her brother Charles home to England where they were brought up by their maternal aunt, Ellen James, with their uncle, Sir Henry James, as formal guardian. Her father died in India when Mary Jane was nine.

The full story of Mary Jane Wilson is most readily available in Portuguese from the recently opened museum set up in her honour in Funchal (see p. 112). In English (and other languages) there is a little book *Sister Wilson Story* (1993) translated from the Portuguese and available from the same place, and an earlier small publication in English *The Invincible Victorian: The Life of Mary Jane Wilson* (Dunphy, c.1950) which I bought on the internet. These accounts also detail her spiritual life and impact; I shall concentrate on the more practical and beneficent side of her work. They also correct the limited information that has hitherto more generally formed the legend around this woman who gave so much to Madeira.

Mary Jane's father had left instructions about his children's upbringing: no expense was to be spared for their education from their limited inheritance and they must be devout. Straitened circumstances meant a peripatetic life for Mary Jane, and a strong will meant difficult relations with Aunt Ellen. By the age of 17, she was not only well-educated but a gifted artist – many accomplished drawings survive but, unfortunately, not of Madeira. She started to move towards Roman Catholicism and converted in 1873 in Boulogne, clutching a little statue of Our Lady of Victories – which was to become the symbol of her Order and work. She also trained as a nurse in France and later worked at St George's Hospital in London.

Mary Jane Wilson landed in Madeira aged 41 as nurse to an invalid, but there is evidence that she had already decided that Madeira was where her wider work would be needed. She wrote home describing it as 'a perfect world, of beauty'. Almost immediately she started her mission on the island, involving herself in religious instruction and the care of poor children and orphans. In 1882, she founded what became St George's Pharmacy, restricted to providing medicine for poor patients and, in 1883, St George's College in the former Palace of São Pedro in Rua da Mouraria (see p. 84). The college has been described as for rich girls, but that seems unlikely, unless it was a means of fundraising at which Mary Jane Wilson became expert. She also set up St Elizabeth Orphanage that year. By then, the Bishop had already asked her to stay and offered support for her work and, in 1884, she set up a religious order at St George's and became a nun. Her first local collaborator was 18-year-old **Amélia Amara de Sá**, later Sister Elizabeth (after St Elizabeth, Queen of Hungary).

In 1889 Mary Jane Wilson agreed to run the dilapidated hospital at Santa Cruz, rebuilding and equipping what was to become the flagship of her Order. In 1895 she was asked to become its matron, and remained so until 1910.

7. Mary Jane Wilson, courtesy of the Franciscan Sisters of Our Lady of Victories

The building still stands in the Rua Irmã Wilson but, in 2001, it was apparently empty and with a melancholy air, the white walls beginning to peel and the shutters closed. On a plaque is the Portuguese inscription: 'Sister Wilson (1840–1916) Founded in

Santa Cruz in 1890 the Order of Franciscan Sisters of Our Lady of Victories.' This commemorated the official seal of approval on her religious Congregation.

A hint of why Santa Cruz might be chosen as a salubrious, yet accessible, place to treat the sick is conveyed by Mrs Roundell visiting it in 1888: 'The inn at Santa Cruz is small, but very comfortable, and people often go there for the sake of the bracing sea air.'

Lazareto (continued)

Now we return in spirit to the Lazareto. At the end of 1905, Sister Wilson was in charge of the Arendrup school at Santo da Serra, which we shall come to. There were signs of smallpox among the poor of Funchal and they began to be confined to the Lazareto. Sister Wilson offered her services to the Governor, who rejected them. Blanche Reid, whose family were friends of Mme Arendrup, recorded events:

A woman from the poorer quarter of [Funchal] was admitted to the Lazaretto suspected of plague. Other suspects followed her into isolation and virtually disappeared from view, as news of the patients was withheld from the populace who started an outcry that no one who went in ever came out again. Rumour was rife as to what happened to them and panic spread, culminating in the sack of the Lazaretto [on 7 January 1906] and the release of the inmates. The town went out of control until restored by a war-ship from Lisbon. To this vessel the head doctor of the Lazaretto made his escape, disguised as a woman. The Lazaretto was left a complete wreck.

Then, in the winter of 1907–08, smallpox, brought by a visiting seaman, spread again, particularly among the seafaring community. When it looked as if an epidemic would sweep the island, Sister Wilson prevailed upon the authorities to allow her swiftly to renovate the damaged Lazareto and to move her Order in to nurse the smallpox patients. It was repaired and equipped in two weeks. Those who had, through fear, avoided inoculation, now trusted the woman who had for so long ministered to the poor, and were willing to be nursed in the Lazareto. Two hundred patients were admitted and more funds poured in as a result of widespread response in the community to

Sister Wilson's fundraising. The epidemic over, she returned to her work among orphans, taking particular and long term responsibility for a lad from the Lazareto who had lost both his parents during the epidemic. She was not only the heroine of the island community but also honoured for her services by the King of Portugal.

Sister Wilson was not the first woman to see smallpox as an island scourge and to try to do something about it, for Fanny Burney Wood wrote of 1838: 'Vaccination is uncommon, nor does the government appear to take any steps to introduce it among the lower classes. Two or three English ladies on the Island vaccinate any of the poor whom they can induce to undergo the operation.' (Who were they?)

A relatively new building now stands on the edge of the Lazareto gorge. It is big enough to be both a training camp for under-privileged youngsters and a residence for the elderly. Although it is rather different from the original, the gorge is still wild and it is possible to imagine Sister Wilson there, as well as in Santa Cruz. We will meet her again in this itinerary and elsewhere (pp. 46–50, 58, 112 and 116).

Machico

Having gone back to the Lazareto only in your mind, now leave Santa Cruz and drive on to Machico. It really is not at all as Fanny Burney Wood described it after a visit in 1839: 'The town of Machico is the dullest and most uninteresting that I have seen in Madeira, and the population the most squalid, dirty and disgusting-looking race of people I ever beheld.'

But do not expect to find much of Anna d'Arfet, the romantic castaway, particularly as more than one guide book suggests that she was buried in Santa Cruz (without giving any more precise details). Today's Capela do Senhor Bom Jesus dos Milagres (Chapel of the Miracles) is more commonly supposed to stand on the spot in Machico where Anna and Robert were buried and where an earlier chapel stood, in place of the cross left by their crew. This is a little confusing if you are following the accounts of earlier travels because, as Ellen Taylor, who visited Madeira in 1880, wrote of the 'Capela de NS da Visitação, commonly called the Misericordia. Here the remains of Machim and Anna d'Arfet were interred; and a very small portion of the cedar cross that originally stood over the grave is shown.' Fanny Burney Wood, visiting the Misericordia 50 years earlier than Ellen, had seen 'on the wall a small glazed frame containing a relic of the cedar cross'. She maintains that the chapel was 'no longer in use in consequence of the river flooding it every winter'. But the guide books are clear about the Chapel of the Miracles; and certainly chapels are commonly built anew on the site of older ones and renamed.

The splinter of the d'Arfet cross is not obviously apparent, it has to be said, and there was no one in the chapel to ask when we went in 2001. There are two sombre paintings showing a violent sea and people, including a woman, coming ashore, but they refer to the storm and flood of 1803 when the chapel and several houses were swept out to sea and a passing ship rescued people and a carved wooden crucifix from the chapel (rebuilt in 1815). A procession commemorating this miracle is held annually on 8 October, and the 9th is a local holiday.

A couple of paintings of Anna and Robert's landfall did exist in what was the Governor's residence (now the São Lourenço Palace and Fort), according to Isabella de França in 1853–54; indeed, she described them in some detail:

One represents the elopement of Robert and Anna from Bristol, painted like an Italian city, with columns, and arches, down to the water's edge. They are embarking on board a ship of the 18th century, and wear the costume of that period. The other shows the lady expiring in the arms of her lover on the beach of Machico, under a tree of Californian dimensions, and the ship sailing away in the distance. The lady is in blue satin, and the gentleman in crimson velvet, with silk stockings; both have their hair powdered, and their dress is, as in the former picture, totally unsoiled by the voyage.

Isabella is patently a non-believer; she even describes the pictures as depicting the 'legend'. Edith Hutcheon mentions the pictures in

1928, but I am reliably informed that they probably went missing when the monarchy fell in 1910.

8. Machico by Lady Susan Harcourt, 1851, from Harcourt, *Sketches in Madeira*

So, imagination is needed as you stand looking out over Machico Bay, though Susan Harcourt's drawing helps. That the islanders themselves continue to take the Machico myth at least semi-seriously is confirmed by a shop called Ana d'Arfet opposite Reid's Hotel in Funchal, and anyone you stop in Machico can direct you to the right chapel (east of the river and towards the headland at its mouth). This may also have been the location of the church outside which Felipa the Prophet was made to stand, though there is more than one church: Nossa Senhora da Conceição was built by **Branca Texeira**, wife of Tristão Vaz, one of the first joint governors of Madeira. He added her name to his and one of the arches of the church incorporates the Texeira coat of arms (see also p. 109).

Another Machico landmark is the Quinta Cristovão where Maria Bianchi Cossart learned about wine from her grandfather (see pp. 14–15). This quinta was originally built, with its own chapel, in 1692 by a descendant of one of the earliest families. And it was from here that Carlo de Bianchi directed most of his business. When Maria travelled from his house in Funchal to Machico, she was carried those nine miles in a hammock borne by two men, just as privileged women had been for centuries in Madeira – a journey she later remembered without pleasure. The younger of the father and son team also remembered those journeys years later, apparently without complaint, though she was a tall lass.

In 1905, the quinta was taken over by Mary Jane Wilson's Order and a convent and school established in it. The Sisters were surprised to find themselves greeted at the pier when they arrived by a large crowd of local people delighted to have their children educated. The school was closed in 1910 but later reopened and is still active – though the quinta's appearance is apparently rather different from the original. To visit it (which I didn't), take the ER108 out of Machico – the most direct way from there to Santo da Serra – and, a few miles on, past a couple of churches, you should ask.

Santo da Serra

Travelling from Santa Cruz in 1854, Isabella de França wrote 'As we returned, the view of Funchal in the most glorious hues of sunset was beautiful indeed!' But I am taking you, instead, inland, to come back the mountain way via Santo da Serra (and Camacha). The full name of the village is Santo António da Serra but, over time, it has become shortened. It stands at 700 metres and was, therefore, an ideal place for a summer residence; it is still lively with quintas, some old, some new.

Following her visit in 1876, Lady Brassey went to Madeira again in 1883, arriving from England to meet her husband and their yacht prior to a voyage round the Atlantic and Caribbean. She writes, in *In Trades, the Tropics and the Roaring Forties* (1885), of visiting Mr Blandy's quinta:

A tolerably long walk brought us to his house at Santo António da Serra, 1,500 feet above Santa Cruz where he and Mrs Blandy met us in an avenue of blue hydrangeas, the adjoining garden being filled with blue agapanthus, pink bella donna-lillies and other flowers. The house itself is a very cosy little place, and the views from the garden are superb.

The house was Quinta António da Serra – also known as Quinta da Junta, Quinta da Serra, Parque do Santo Serra, or Quinta Blandy. The property was bought and the house built by the original wine merchant John Blandy in 1843 and belonged, thereafter, to various members of the family. Annie Brassey is probably talking of Richard Ridpath Blandy and his wife **Ada Eliza Penfold** (1852–1908). The entrance to the quinta can be found 200 metres from the church down a cobbled track, still lined with agapanthus and hydrangea and, depending on the time of year, camellias and azaleas. The pink house is now government offices and not open to the public, but the gardens are. They include a children's play area, an enclosure with goats, deer and wild ponies, tennis courts and a crazy golf course. Beyond, a path winds down through tangy-smelling trees to the Miradouro dos Ingleses from where, on a clear day, you can see Porto Santo.

There is also a path called Fanny's walk. This is named after Richard's sister **Fanny Blandy** (Frances Anna 1837–1916). She met the scientist Sir William Thomson (created Lord Kelvin in 1892) when, in 1865, he was part of the team laying the transatlantic cable. She understood his work and used to signal to him from the family's quinta at Santa Luzia (see p. 141). He returned to marry her in 1874, following the death of his wife, and they spent some time in Madeira in subsequent years.

Leaving Quinta Junta, you drive down the main street and, somewhere there, at the beginning of the twentieth century, Miss Turner managed a tea-room serving Ceylon tea and hot buttered toast.

Now, drive westwards and, about two miles out, when you are long past any buildings and think you must have missed the turning, you will see a narrow road on your left, happily signposted Estrada Mary Jane Wilson. Drive down this some way, avoiding anxiety at how far it seems – you are now in the back of beyond. If in doubt, ask a farmer, who may have Anglo-Saxon looks: '*Capela, faz favor.*'

You are looking for the Arendrup School which, when you finally reach it, will be obvious: it is boldly marked, and there is another Mary Jane Wilson signpost.

Edith Arendrup (née Courtauld, 1846–1934) was an Englishwoman who, in 1873, married a Danish officer attached to the Egyptian army and lived in Cairo during the three years of her marriage. When in 1876 her husband was killed in battle, leaving her pregnant, Edith returned to England after her son, Axel, was born and took responsibility, too, for two stepdaughters.

She was not destitute – she came from a Huguenot-Unitarian family which had built up a successful silk and crepe business. At some stage, which the author of the booklet *Triumph Over Tragedy* (Milward, 1991) was unable to determine, she converted to Roman Catholicism. She regarded France as her second home and that may have been a factor. Settled in Wimbledon, just outside London, she found that the only place of worship was distant and set up a chapel in the house; but that was not enough. Her mother had died when she was nine, now her father died leaving her his fortune and she began the moves which eventually led to the building of the Sacred Heart Church in Wimbledon which she funded.

But all the while, she was bothered by the fragility of Axel's health, and began taking him to Madeira or Tenerife in the winter. In Madeira he was looked after by an English nurse – Mary Jane Wilson. With so much in common, the two women became lifelong friends. What is more, Edith had the money and the will to give; Sister Wilson had the projects. Axel, unfortunately, died in Madeira in 1896; the projects flourished. Madeira inspired one of Edith Arendrup's best-known canvases for, until the death of her husband, she had aspired to become a professional artist. She eventually entered a secular religious order.

The parish priest of Santo da Serra had approached Sister Wilson in 1898 for help because there was no opportunity for the education

9. Portratit of recently widowed Edith Arendrup, 1876, from Milward, *Triumph Over Tragedy*

of his flock in the scattered hamlets around; what was more, the 'Methodists' were much stronger in the area. Sister Wilson's response was to approach Edith Arendrup for financial help. Once the school in a convent was built, the 'Methodist minister', with whom Sister Wilson was friendly, informed her with some bewilderment, 'I am having very good results in some places but in Santo da Serra, where there is a church and House, things are very awkward and slack. Some Irish person built a Catholic Church and school practically next door to mine and took over most of my flock.' She did not enlighten him.

With the revolution of 1910, and the closure of religious houses (see pp. 58–9), Sister Wilson had to think fast. Realising that the building of the House had been financed by Mme Arendrup, a British subject, she waited till the order for dispersal came and immediately ordered the Sisters to hoist the Union Jack. They changed their religious habits for secular clothing and continued teaching.

In this quiet corner Sister Wilson planned to spend the rest of her days, living there between 1911 and 1916. Her interest in gardening was given full rein; she wrote home in 1911: 'The garden is beginning to look so nice. There are more than 200 Arum lilies in bloom, white azaleas, 3 different camellias, giant daisies, purple and white irises, daffodils, jonquils, violets and 4 different kinds of roses, besides other kinds of plants.'

Today, there is a more modern school attached to the original chapel and little convent. But the garden is still there and, stretched along the garden wall in the blue and white *azulejos* (tiles) so characteristic of Madeira (and Portugal), is a portrait of Sister Wilson and two of her texts.

This itinerary now takes you back to the main road and to Camacha but we had two visits to this area and, on the second, having come from Camacha, and our regular driver being intrigued by signs of a new linking section to the road, we followed the narrow road spiralling down the ravine to the coast, to Santa Cruz. Though the road provides its moments of anxiety, you spot the hamlets whose children attend the school, and the views are impressive.

Camacha

Camacha has for a century and a half been the home of wicker weaving and where foreign residents of Madeira retired during the hot summer months. It was not a place to go to in March; as Isabella de França wrote of visiting friends there: 'The rain set in again as soon as we arrived, and the cold was so severe, that we all clustered round the good fires ...'

So pleasant a refuge was it in summer that **Flora Shaw** (1852–1929), first Colonial Editor of *The Times* (of London), chose to spend her honeymoon there in 1902. She stayed for a month at Reid's Hotel (then known as Reid's New Hotel). There she was joined by Sir Frederick Lugard and they married quietly at the British Consulate on 11 June. Then, in the cool of the afternoon, they drove up to Camacha to a quinta they had been lent on a mountain overlooking the sea and with a big garden surrounded by woods.

This is said in her records to be the quinta of Mr Graham but that must be Dr Michael Grabham, perhaps the best known of Camacha's expatriates. He was married to Fanny Blandy's sister **Mary Anne** (b. 1843, named after her mother, Mary Anne Symonds Blandy). The fate of their quinta – Quinta Camacha – once so full of life and its owner so renowned – is rather typical of that of many, so large and expensive to keep up and run in changed times. The family sold the quinta in 1910. During the Second World War it was used to house refugees from Gibraltar. By the 1950s it had become a rundown hotel-pension where films, mostly Westerns, were shown once a week and where chickens fluttered and squawked when disturbed in dilapidated courtyards and corridors.

Today, if you drive round Camacha looking intently for the past, you will see two padlocked gates on the outskirts guarding an overgrown and abandoned property and, through unloved undergrowth, you can just discern the remnants of the house which was badly damaged by fire in 1998.

From there Flora and her new husband left for Nigeria, where he was the first high commissioner and, in 1907, they moved to Hong Kong where he was to be governor, an appointment as much of her as of him.

Other than this abandoned quinta, identifying these properties in Camacha today presents a problem. Isabella de França had written of arriving there from Funchal in September 1853:

> As we approach Camacha we find a good deal of purple heath and banks are overhung with brambles and honeysuckle, giving quite an English appearance to the scene ... after passing some cottages, and two handsome quintas, belonging to English Merchants, we emerged on the Achada of Camacha. Achada signifies a piece of level ground on the side of a mountain, and this, were it not so situated, has all the appearance of an English common. A few yards further down a narrow lane, brought us to our destination.

She goes on to describe the house and garden of their friend's quinta. Her editor in 1969 determined that their destination was the home of William Burton Penfold, which he calls Quinta da Achada, and another source, Noel Cossart, also lists a Penfold quinta of that name there. But the family also had a quinta of that name to the north-west of Funchal – which we shall visit in 'Flowers, Gardens and Walks' (pp. 127–31) – and no one I have talked to, nor any of the local people our driver talked to in Camacha as we searched determinedly, had ever heard of the Penfolds' Quinta da Achada there. A mystery still to be solved, please!

But wicker weaving thrives as much as ever. Just as the women doing embroidery at home (see 'Bella Phelps and Embroidery', pp. 28–32) might be helped by their men when they were over-stretched so, in basket weaving, which was said to be mens' work, the women often became involved. Ellen Taylor wrote of her 1880–81 visit to Camacha:

> This is quite a village of wicker chairs and basket-makers; they work at their cottage doors, and we overtook many women carrying piles of chairs and little tea-tables into Funchal. This branch of industry has increased considerably of late years, owing to the Cape packets taking away large quantities.

But the women did not only carry finished products to market. There are archival photographs showing women, as well as men, posing with bundles of willow and one firsthand account of 1924 (Alan Lethbridge) describes women taking heavy bundles of stripped willow into Funchal and selling them to manufacturers. Once again, as with embroidery, as time went by home work was done hand-in-hand with 'factory' processes. What is more, at a particular factory, the writer's guide was a 'forewoman' with strong arms who had been involved in the process for 25 years – a woman who had obvious respect from the 'boys' under her control. In Camacha, this same informant noticed communal work – men, women and children – done in 'artels' conveying aspects of 'trade unionism'.

Not everyone was in a position to look that closely. In 1928 Edith Hutcheon elaborated on 'the finest osier the world produces':

One sees it everywhere – fields of it, it lines the banks of the streams, grows in gardens round the picturesque peaked, thatched huts and homes of the peasants, whom it is interesting to watch as they work in the open air, deftly and swiftly fashioning the willow into the well-known wicker chairs, sofas, tables, and baskets for which there is such demand, and which are bought in vast quantities by the passengers of steamers which put in to Funchal. One sees the finished articles in the town, overflowing the shops on to the pavements. Stacks of it rocking on the water as the boats and launches make for the steamers in the bay; one meets it on the mountain roads carried on the heads of women and girls, who do wonderful balancing feats with their unwieldy loads, or piled up on rough sledges drawn by women and boys down the steep cobbled tracks into Funchal.

Edith Hutcheon saw mainly beauty in Madeira; Lady Emmeline Stuart-Wortley was differently inclined; she wrote in 1851 of a trip to the Grand Curral:

We passed many of the peasants, among whom were a large number of women, most of them bearing huge and heavy loads upon their heads, unpleasant turban tubs, or piles of various articles, and towers of baskets – and almost all of them, poor creatures, looking old. They work extremely hard, and their food is scanty and bad.

Edith Hutcheon's rosier view most likely had as much to do with social progress in Madeira as Lady Emmeline's sourness revealed her need to be provocative. It is not easy to find biographical details of **Edith Hutcheon** but her travelling companion, to whom she dedicates her book, was **Dame Henrietta Barnett** (1851–1936) who had seen plenty of deprivation in London over the years. There, she worked with Octavia Hill among the poor of Marylebone and later, with her own husband, founded Toynbee Hall in Whitechapel. It was also she who realised a dream in the creation of Hampstead Garden Suburb which, from 1907, consciously embraced all sections of the community.

In 1953, Elizabeth Nicholas thought she brought the wicker story up to date where women were concerned:

... On average the industry employs about 5,000 people. It is interesting that, until quite recently, it has been purely a masculine preserve; one might think that basket making would not be beyond the strength of country women but, in fact, I am told it is very heavy work and suited only to men. A start has however been made in the instruction and employment of women in the manufacture of small baskets and mats, which at the moment sell very well in America.

By 1961, young Camacha women in workshops of six to eight were adept at making the wicker covers for wine bottles and today basketwork is still available everywhere, particularly in large showrooms in Camacha. (Palm weaving on Porto Santo is the preserve of the women of Serra de Fora.)

As for the countrywomen, my most vivid impression of them, on our first visit, was of gaily dressed, bescarfed and booted, rather taciturn sellers of vegetables and fruit at the side of the road. They were a great boon, allowing one to stock up in January on such good and healthy produce as tree tomatoes (known as *tomate Ingles*), guavas and lady's finger bananas, as well as giving the marvellous mountains and valleys a human focus. This may be your first experience of Madeira's fine and distinctive scenery and thus has a special value.

The road between Camacha and Funchal is still much as it was when Isabella de França passed that way 150 years ago and wrote (travelling this time from Funchal):

Above the Palheiro, the character of the country becomes totally altered; vineyards disappear and are replaced by woods of pine and chestnut trees, the soil is red with grey rocks cropping out here and there; thin wiry grass, or close rich moss, clothe the hill sides where trees do not grow, but the broom with its profusion of golden flowers shining in the sun, is almost too brilliant to look upon.

My own memory is of mimosa rather than broom but the effect is the same. There are two kinds of mimosa on the island, both originally from Australia: one, the bright yellow ball, blooms in January; the other, more creamy, in March/April. Before you reach your final destination of Funchal, there is the Quinta do Palheiro (eight kilometres out), the history and gardens of which will be discussed in 'Flowers, Gardens and Walks' (pp. 154–9).

Waterfront (Funchal) from the Old Town

Rua de Santa Maria, Autonomy Square, São Lourenço, Casa do Turista, Marina Centre, Santa Catarina Gardens and Chapel, Quinta Vigia (formerly Quinta das Angústias), Hospício, Orphanage, Old Quinta Vigia, The Hotel Savoy, Ribeiro Seco, Reid's Palace

If you like to promenade, Funchal waterfront is the place and one end is also where Funchal's history begins.

Stand with your back to Nossa Senhora do Socorro and, gazing out to sea, you can begin to recapture the past. The large, old, end house nearest the church is where we stayed, chez Dona Vitorina, on our second visit using information from guide books. The welcome was warm, the facilities those for the budget traveller. If that is you, there are large separate rooms with a shared bathroom, or a couple of self-contained flats. Eschew the ground floor one without a view and plump for that on the first floor from where you can see the street, the sea, and the best and earliest jacaranda tree in Funchal. This accommodation is at the other end of the spectrum from the luxury of Reid's Palace where we stayed with my mother on our first visit and for two days at the end of our second and which comes, coincidentally, at the other end of this waterfront itinerary.

Rua de Santa Maria

Dona Vitorina's best selling point, apart from comparative economy, is location. So now, wearing thick soled shoes against the sharp cobbles, walk westwards along Rua de Santa Maria towards the centre of Funchal. (If you were to walk eastwards you would, in half an hour or so, reach the Lazareto). It is here that the first artisans set up shop in the fifteenth century and where ungentrified workshops and houses still prevail. Many of the old dwellings have been converted into small, good value restaurants, bringing a boost and adding a sparkle to a previously poor area. If you want to hear fado, the haunting Portuguese singing, there are, in 2004, two fine women exponents at Arsenio's, one of whom sings and records with her husband, waiter-manager of the restaurant where the food complements the singing.

Half-way along the Rua de Santa Maria, when you have drunk your fill of the picturesque, turn left and down to the waterfront, passing on your left the São Tiago Fort, part of which is now the Museum of Contemporary Art. Although I was disappointed not to find women appropriately represented, I understand they do have exhibitions of women artists. An important example is Martha Teles (1930–2001).

Autonomy Square

Walk along the prom which was just as popular as a public walk in the nineteenth century. Emily Shore wrote on 6 January 1839, 'We went first to the Esplanade, or, according to its more correct though ridiculous name, the Praça Academica.' Today, you will pass the beginning of the cable car up to Monte (see pp. 142–9). Stop when you reach Praça da Autonomia (Autonomy Square). There, perched high on a column, is the womanly figure of Autonomy, one arm raised, stark and effective against the amphitheatre of hills rising behind Funchal.

Autonomy is of significance to Madeirans. In 1974, revolution ended years of fascist, centralised government from Lisbon. On 1 July 1976, Madeira achieved autonomy and it now has its own Assembly and Government. Relations between Lisbon and Funchal may work smoothly but some Portuguese visitors still regard the islanders as country cousins with funny accents – one young mainland woman regretting the absence on her holiday of expected 'hula hula girls' and other exoticisms. The spaciousness and backdrop of the Praça in which the column stands reinforce the significance of the sculpture and the concept it represents.

On the westernmost corner is the Customs House leaning out from the wall of which are the figures of a woman holding an olive branch in one hand and a cogged wheel in the other and a man holding the rod of Asclepius and a galleon. In front of that building, on the

10. View of Funchal by Emily Smith, 1843, from Smith, *A Panoramic View of the City of Funchal*

waterfront, is a thick, square column faced with figures – one of them female – signifying gratitude to the business people who have helped make Madeira prosperous. Madeira is full of sculptures, old and new, many of them, like Autonomy, enhancing the scene.

São Lourenço

As you continue along the front, you come to the Marina and Port on your left. Go down some steps to find out about boat and other trips. On your right, across the road (Avenida do Mar), is the Fort and Palace of São Lourenço. It is from here that the paintings of Anna d'Arfet and Robert Machim have gone missing (see p. 44) but, more significantly, Mary Jane Wilson stayed here. In 1910 Portugal became a republic and Sister Wilson's life was turned on its head as, with the Proclamation, all religious communities were to be closed down and foreign members of them expelled. Once again Blanche Reid recorded events:

The overthrow of the monarchy and proclamation of the Republic were marked by much violence against the Church and its institutions, in the course of which Sister Mary Wilson was arrested, brought to Funchal and imprisoned. The 'heathens', as our family called the local anti-religious revolutionaries, kept her under interrogation for several days despite all that anyone, my father [Alfred Reid] in particular, could do to convince them that the poor lady was entirely non-political. Nothing that my father said would persuade them to let him even go in to see her, so in the end he had to create a great furore and resort to violence, forcing his way into the room in which she was, and refusing to leave without her.

Sister Wilson remained in the fortress between 14 and 18 October. Unfortunately, that part of the complex is still confined to the military and, although I have made enquiries – as, apparently, have several nuns – it has not proved possible to establish where she was held, let alone to see the place.

Her first act on being detained was to send telegrams to the Superiors of the Order's establishments directing them to change into civilian dress and to send the Sisters to the safety of their homes. From the fortress, she was deported. Before leaving for England dressed, of course, in her habit, she pronounced to the Sisters who had come to say goodbye, 'All we have to do now is collect up the bags and depart. Anyone who is going to cry had better not come to the quayside.' She boarded calmly and, on her arrival in England, went to stay with her widowed sister-in-law. She wrote constant encouragement and advice to Madeira, meanwhile agitating to be allowed to return. Against all the odds, she was successful, and arrived back on 11 November 1911. She went to live at Santo da Serra. She was now 71 and might have thought there was little more she could do (see pp. 50 and 112).

Casa do Turista

Just past the São Lourenço is the Casa do Turista, a charming place to buy mementoes of Madeira and Portugal, including embroidery, wickerwork, wines and ceramics, all set out in constantly changing rooms and table displays. This innovative way of selling was devised by Maria-Luísa Bianchi (née Ramos) who, in 1956, needing a job and outlet for latent artistic talent, sought the support of her father to find and finance a 'small place'. She developed her project over the next 40 years, paying attention to every artistic detail and enhancing the arrangements with flowers brought down on Mondays from Quinta do Palheiro by Mildred Blandy (see pp. 157–8). Maria-Luísa sold the business in 1995. She is an early example of the increasing number of women entrepreneurs on the island.

Marina Centre

Not far past Casa do Turista is the last of the prom on your left; beyond is the container port and, to your right, the road leads you into a tunnel – to be avoided. You could have lunch now – the cafes that line the waterfront, though touristy, are perfectly acceptable

11. São Lourenço from the Lazareto by Emily Smith, 1842, courtesy of Quinta das Cruzes Museum

(we tried the last place and ate espada fillet in muffin with salad). You could even call it a day if walking on the flat is what you prefer. Otherwise, the next move is to turn up the incline before the tunnel road, with the Marina shopping complex on your right. For centuries the old Lazareto stood here and, some time later, the Quinta das Fontes which became the first hotel of William George and Margaret Dewey Reid (see p. 113). The painting by Emily Smith of the São Lourenço from the Lazareto, more than many others, shows how things have changed in 150 years.

Santa Catarina Gardens and Chapel

Opposite the side of the Marina Centre, further up the incline, and very obvious, are the Santa Catarina Gardens. The name is usually spelt out in flowers. Go up the path towards the chapel on the site of the one built by Constança Rodrigues in 1425 (see p. 4). On the left of the path, you pass the supine torso of a woman – not one of the most appealing sculptures, particularly since there is no indication of what this rather brutal object signifies.

And so to the locked chapel, such a sad, neglected sight, though the view from the terrace is fine. If you failed to eat earlier, or are just thirsty, as you continue westwards round the gardens, you should come to a cafe which serves the fresh juice of any number of fruit. Then skirt the cafe towards the road (Avenida do Infante, a continuation of Avenida Arriaga) and you come to the gates of the very pink Quinta Vigia, the residence of Madeira's President.

Quinta Vigia (formerly Quinta das Angústias)

This is both a confusing and a historic quinta – confusing because it used to be called Quinta das Angústias and, towards the end of the nineteenth century, Quinta Lambert; and another quinta just beyond, now a casino-hotel, was called the Quinta Vigia. So confusing is it that some commentators mistake who stayed where.

The day we went, entry was delayed until 2.00 p.m., but that seems to depend on official activities. In any case, you can only visit the gardens and the little chapel built into the body of the house. Walk through the formal gardens to the end of the terrace overlooking the sea, past the rather gruesomely small cages of big exotic birds. There, at the end, you will find 'Dona Guiomar's *Mirante*'. This is not the belvedere of an eighteenth century lady of leisure but the lookout of a woman with work to do concerning the comings and goings of her ships. The small two-storeyed building appears to be the only part of the Quinta das Angústias intact from Guiomar's day (see pp. 11–13).

The nineteenth century Quinta das Angústias had more than one interesting visitor, but fewer than are sometimes ascribed to it. After her death in 1839, the family of Emily Shore stayed here for a few months; you will meet her in more detail in the next itinerary (see pp. 74–8). Some sources – particularly biographies – have Dowager Queen Adelaide of England staying here, but it seems clear that she spent the winter of 1847–48 at the original Quinta Vigia. Other sources say the same of Empress Elizabeth of Austria in 1860.

It was, though, to the Quinta das Angústias that the Dowager Empress of Brazil brought her 21-year-old daughter Dona Maria Amélia in 1852, and where the Princess died of consumption five months later (see also pp. 27–8).

Hospício

Across the main road, and only slightly further down the hill, is a gate guarded by two venerable and intertwined dragon trees which leads into the grounds of the Hospício Princesa Dona Maria Amélia which Empress Amélia had built to celebrate the short life of her daughter (see also pp. 27–8). **Ellen Taylor**, who was in Madeira between January 1880 and January 1881, was most impressed by the Hospício. In *Madeira: Its Scenery and How to See It, with Letters of a Year's Residence* (1882; 1889) she quotes from a letter home:

... The building ... is large and very well built, standing in a most commanding situation on an eminence overlooking the town, though only just out of it, and surrounded by terraces and gardens filled with rare and beautiful trees, shrubs and flowers planted with great taste, and some really green turf dividing the beds ... One of the sisters received us very courteously, and took us all over the beautiful building and the adjoining orphanage. The Hospício is always full in the winter, and the patients look very clean and comfortable, but most of them seemed very ill indeed. They have every care taken of them, and it is impossible that any poor sick people should be better looked after or more kindly treated. After paying the Sister Superior a short visit, we came away very much pleased and interested.

The gardens, which are described in more detail under 'Flowers, Gardens and Walks' (pp. 126–7), are open to the public. Today the Hospício is a centre for the elderly: some live there permanently and may be ailing, some short term, some visit it by day. If you want to see inside, choose an appropriate time – that is, not when frail people may be having a siesta. But, all being well, if you push open the door and say '*Capela faz favor*', a passing carer or auxiliary will take you up the imposing staircase, past the plaque dedicating the building to the Princess, to the chapel. Dominating the small room is the marble Madonna donated by Archduke Maximilian of Austria who had been engaged to the Princess.

Orphanage

In 1880, an orphanage was built alongside the Hospício, also run by the Sisters of the Order of St Vincent de Paul. It is the white painted building on the main road just to your left as you face the Hospício. It is not really open to the public but, if you are keen to follow historical trails, no objection is raised if you poke a discreet nose inside.

In her 'How to See It' section, Ellen Taylor writes of the Orphanage:

... Orphan girls are trained most thoroughly to every sort of household work, that they may be fit to enter domestic service. Needle work, cooking, laundry and housemaid's duties are well taught ...Visitors are glad to avail themselves of this, and the money thus earned is a great addition to the orphanage funds.

Ellen sent her own laundry, and that of her companion, to the Orphanage and judged it 'very well done'. That's as may be in 1880. In 1854, Isabella de França describes in some detail how laundry is done on the rocks at the river's edge with no soap and much bashing and twisting – a process which could still be seen in the late twentieth century.

Ellen also tells us that, having obtained further funds, the Order built an infant school where 'every day from eighty to a hundred children are taught. The very poorest having their dinner given them.' As for her companion, after a year in Madeira, Ellen was able to write home, 'D is quite another creature, and has regained much of her lost strength.' Biographical details of Ellen are lacking.

By 1908, the Sisters of St Vincent de Paul had withdrawn from the Orphanage and their place was taken by Sister Wilson's Franciscan Order with Sister Elizabeth as Superior. When the events of 1910 occurred, the Sisters at the Lazareto were detained and driven in public through the streets to jeers. To avoid this, the Sisters at the Orphanage melted away overnight, causing understandable upset to their little charges. They returned in 1926 following another revolution. Today, if you venture inside and up the staircase, you will find suddenly before you a huge photographic portrait of Sister Wilson and three small children.

Old Quinta Vigia

Now, cross back over Avenida do Infante and walk further up the incline away from today's Quinta Vigia. There on your left is the Carlton Park Hotel on the site of the original Quinta Vigia. It is somewhat startling to find, in the public space in front of the hotel, a life size statue of **Empress Elizabeth of Austria** (1837–1898), Sisi, as she is affectionately known in Madeira, in a ballgown. She stayed at the quinta in 1860 to recuperate either from a physical illness or because her marriage to Franz Joseph, which took place in 1854, was going through a bad patch. There are also glass fronted cases on stands nearby containing articles about her stay. She arrived on the Royal Yacht *Victoria and Albert* from England and created quite a stir because she was so beautiful, elegant and charming.

Mrs Foote, who arrived at much the same time, on her way to Lagos where her husband was British Consul, notes in *Recollections of Central America and the West Coast of Africa* (1869) that the Empress made Madeira fashionable for the 'Germans' and adds, 'I used frequently to see her driving about in her ox carriage, which mode of conveyance caused her, I heard, great amusement on first arriving in Funchal.' An ox cart had met her at the seashore on her arrival, 'at which her gravity quite gave way'. It appeared, Mrs Foote continued, 'that in Austria condemned criminals are always taken to the scaffold in vehicles drawn by oxen'.

At the base of Sisi's statue are inscribed in Portuguese the words, 'I would like to leave this world like a bird, like a trail of smoke.' She was assassinated by an anarchist on the shores of Lake Geneva.

An earlier guest at the quinta was Elizabeth's brother-in-law, the Archduke Maximilian of Austria. He had already visited Madeira in 1852 not long before the death of his fiancée, Princess Maria Amélia of Brazil. Now, in 1859, he returned with his wife, **Charlotte of Belgium** (1840–1927). They had been married for two years and had spent them in Trieste where his brother, the Emperor Franz Joseph, had foisted him on the people as Viceroy. Their stay in Trieste had been grisly: by the end they could hardly appear in public without provoking hostility. They needed a break but Maximilian soon left 19-year-old Charlotte at Quinta Vigia while he set off (either to South Africa or Brazil, depending on your source) to do some research. She spent the winter travelling round Madeira and wrote a book – *Un Hiver à Madère* (published in 1863 in Vienna) which I have failed to find. She also did some drawings, one of them a view of Funchal which illustrates a chapter on quintas in Maria Lamas' *Arquipélago da Madeira* (1956).

In 1864 the couple were palmed off on the Mexicans as Emperor Maximilian and Empress Carlotta. He was to be executed there by firing squad three years later and she, returning to Europe just before to try and raise help, was to live for another 60 years and die in a mental asylum.

The Hotel Savoy

The next hotel on your left is the is the rather longer-established Savoy. In 1902, José Dias Nascimento acquired Quinta Sheffield then on this site and developed it into the Hotel Royal. In 1926, he started to build what became the Savoy and it opened in 1929. Dias had six children with his wife **Eugenia Silva** – the one that concerns us is their daughter **Adelaide Dias Nascimento** (1898–1988). She married a Portuguese army officer (Vasco Paiva Brites) 15 years her junior and they had no children. Though sons inherited the Savoy and they and grandsons of the founders took over the running, Adelaide – always called *Menina* or Miss Adelaide in the hotel – was the power behind the throne.

While Reid's was where British VIPs stayed, the Savoy hosted the Portuguese elite from the mainland and it was, because of Adelaide, one long party. She would regularly have twelve to dinner and then take them up to the night club – she did that until she was 88, considering it part of the hotel's public relations – but she was also in her office by day. She died at 90 – after being in a coma for two years – 15 days after the hotel was sold.

Ribeiro Seco

The two grandes dames of Madeira's hotel industry are separated by the Ribeiro Seco – the starting point for the road to Câmara de Lobos that Dowager Queen Adelaide helped to fund, ostensibly to help the poor fisherfolk (see p. 17). Mrs Foote wrote of 1860 that 'The fashionable promenade had lately been completed' and described it as 'a broad, smooth, civilised looking road, winding round the edge of the cliffs [which] commands lovely and extensive views'. She continues, 'Here at sunset, are to be seen all the elite of Funchal, mostly on horseback, but a few also lumbering along in the ox-carriage. Pedestrians are few and far between.' Blanche Reid notes how, in later years, this being the only flat bit of road, it lent itself to the horse and carriage for a promenade which she did with her aunt, wearing veils over their 'smart hats'. Isabella de França's paintings (see pp. 36 and 143), illustrate other modes of transport – the palanquin and the ox sledge. In other paintings, she shows the ubiquitous hammock.

The problems of transport, fresh air and exercise for expatriate women in earlier days are best summed up by an extract from the diary, published only on the internet, of **Elizabeth Macquarie** (née Campbell of Airds, 1778–1835). Travelling in 1809 to her husband's new post as Governor of New South Wales, Australia, she spent a week in Madeira, her movements much constrained by sickness after a month at sea, and wrote of the beauty, romance and relief of arriving. But, by the time she had been on shore a few days, she complained of 'the want of air, and great heat; the total exclusion from all kinds of exercise, from the hardness of the roads; which are very steep, and paved with small stones.'

Cross now over the bridge and you come, again on your left, to the pink walls of our next historic hotel.

Reid's Palace

The early days of the Reid family in Madeira are described in the next but one itinerary (see pp. 113–14). It was only later that they began to build what is now Reid's Palace hotel (known more famously just as Reid's), on the cliffs west of Funchal; indeed, William George died (in 1888) before its completion by his sons William and Alfred. The first stage opened in 1891 and it was completed 1900–01. One of the earliest visitors, in 1891, was Empress Elizabeth of Austria recovering from the death of her son at Mayerling. Blanche Reid, whose mother Clara was not only much involved in the functioning of the hotel but also the Empress's confidante, writes:

The Empress's suite in the hotel opened on to a verandah overlooking the man o' war anchorage, where ships of the Royal Navy lay during one of the annual visits of the Channel Squadron. Every morning while there the Fleet fired a royal salute and hoisted the Austrian flag with the band playing, for which Elizabeth would stand on her verandah, looking out to the ships in acknowledgement, her magnificent hair hanging down her back in two great plaits.

Reid's closed during the First World War. When it opened again, an early visitor was Elizabeth's successor as **Empress of Austria, Zita** (granddaughter of Dom Miguel I of Portugal), who accompanied her husband Karl into exile in Madeira in 1921. He died within a year at Quinta Gordon at Monte where he is buried in the church (see pp. 148–9). In years thereafter, she would return to Madeira dressed in 'trailing widow's weeds' to visit his grave.

Today's management maintains the high standard that the Reids must have set in Madeira over a hundred years ago but, in between, there was obviously time for hiccups, for the British consul in 1906 wrote of the New Hotel (its name then): 'If only he would take a little trouble to ensure proper management and decent cooking. At present the management is in the hands of wholly incompetent women who ... devote what time they can spare from flirtation (and worse) with visitors to the neglect of their duties.' (Was **Daisy Esplay** Reid's housekeeper in 1908 involved? Or was she a necessary replacement?) As well as introducing the family through earlier hotels in the centre of town, there is more about them under 'Botanical Gardens' in 'Flowers, Gardens and Walks' (pp. 149–53).

If you have followed this itinerary through to this long end – climbing slightly but definitely since the Marina Centre – and you are not staying there, now would be your chance to have tea at Reid's – long a fashionable and pleasant experience. You need to book in advance.

Rua da Carreira (Funchal)
Westwards and Northwards

Rua da Carreira, Cecilia Zino's House, English Church, British Cemetery, Slavery, Municipal Museum, Frederico de Freitas Museum, Santa Clara Convent, Quinta das Cruzes Museum

Rua da Carreira

If you start this Funchal ramble at the easy meeting point of the Cathedral, walk along Avenida Arriaga and turn right (north) up Avenida Zarco. Turning left into Rua da Carreira, you come first, on your left, to the English Bookshop in a pleasant courtyard with a cafe and, upstairs, the Vicentes Photographic Museum – the whole complex is known as the Pâtio. It suggests what a commonplace nineteenth century architectural feature must have been like (see also p. 71).

On 9 January 1839, Emily Shore wrote of Rua da Carreira, near enough to where she was staying for her to have the energy to reach it, that

[It] seems to be one of the principal streets of Funchal; it is really handsome, spite of the irregularity of the building, for there are no two houses alike in Funchal, and certainly it is marvellously clean. It is easy to see where a stream ran down the middle; it is now covered over with a perforated stone here and there, and gratings which lift up. The shops of Funchal are mean dark holes; nothing is displayed at the windows, and the name of the owner, instead of being placed conspicuously above the door, is written in insignificant characters on a small board hung out on a stick a few feet from the ground. The commonest notice on these boards is 'Pão Vinho Bom' [Good Bread and Wine], often abridged into 'P.V.B.'

There is still more than a whiff of the first part of her description only; it certainly does not resemble the Funchal described by **Maria Riddell**, later a close friend of Robert Burns who admired both her and her writing. She was the first woman traveller to write about her visit (very brief) in 1788. Her book – *Voyage to the Madeira etc Isles* (1792; 1802) was published, with Burns' help, under the name Maria

R—— although she was travelling as Maria Woodley just before her marriage. She stayed in the house of Mr Bissett, a wine merchant, and wrote: 'The town is dirty and shabby, though by no means small; the houses are mean and irregular; the streets are dreadfully ill-paved and extremely narrow.' One of the strongest impressions today, certainly of the town centre, is of a particularly clean and well-ordered place, the well-preserved historical architecture of which has a distinctive allure.

The diplomatic wife **Ann Bridge** (Lady O'Malley, 1889–1974), in the chapter 'Madeira and the Azores' in *A Selective Traveller in Portugal* (1949; 1958), sums up Funchal's architecture, no doubt influenced by the many fine cities she had known:

What there is has charm, rather the charm of modest simplicity than of magnificence. Indeed, the contrast between the modesty of buildings and the extravagant luxuriance of the vegetation is one of the outstanding features of Madeira.

Elizabeth of Austria less kindly remarked of Funchal in 1860, 'If I had known what it was like I would have gone elsewhere', but that referred to its inability to take her out of herself, rather than its cleanliness or aesthetics. While the air was invigorating, she accepted, there was more to life than breathing.

If you continue northwards from where Avenida Zarco meets Rua da Carreira, Rua das Pretas joins Calçada de Santa Clara by the São Pedro Church. Up that quite steep street are the Municipal Museum, the Frederico de Freitas Museum, the Santa Clara Convent and the Quinta das Cruzes Museum. You could go straight up there but leave it till later or another time and, instead, go along Rua da Carreira – a truly delightful street – to where, on your right, the Rua do Quebra Costas (sometimes called Travessa da Bella Vista) also runs steeply north. Stop there on your left. Isabella de França's 1969 editor says that house was then number 11, but it is certainly not now – it is 215 – though it could well have been where Isabella stayed. Now picture her as she arrives in 1853 with her Madeiran husband. She wrote of that first impression:

At last we arrived at our hotel, in the Carreira, the principal street in Funchal. A very large, heavy door stood open, leading into the Patio, a sort of entrance hall, level with and paved like the street. Nearly all the best houses have this Patio, into which people on horseback, or in palanquims, ride at once, and dismount under cover, at the foot of the stairs. We alighted at the door, and went up a flight of stone steps, at the top of which our Hostess appeared, and led us to our apartments ...

... From our drawing room windows we looked first into our own garden, and those of the neighbouring houses, full of the most brilliant flowers. These gardens are bounded by the old City wall; beyond are vineyards, cottages, quintas, the Chapel of the Cemetery, with its gateway, standing in a grove of cypress, cane plantations, chestnut and other luxuriant foliage, amongst which the stupendous leaves of the banana stand out magnificently ...

... Our bedroom has two windows commanding the same view as the drawing room, and another looking to the mountains ... Here we saw another part of the City. Immediately in front was the English Church, & several houses, of which some had beautiful gardens. Above was the Convent of Sta. Clara, and beyond it the Quinta of the Cruzes with its large garden full of tall forest trees, many of very rare species.

Cecilia Zino's House

Isabella de França could not have set the scene better for today. Though the luxuriant foliage has been constrained by development and the city walls have gone, the first house on the right, at the bottom of Rua do Quebra Costas, with fine trees, particularly a towering palm, and a high wall, still looks as if Isabella had it in her sights. Today it is owned by a branch of the Zinos – a family of Genoese origin and long-established British citizenship which came to Madeira via Morocco and Gibraltar in the mid-nineteenth century.

Cecilia Rose Zino (married to William Clifford) died young in that house in 1953 and her family used her estate to set up a Foundation which they administer and which funds the work of Dominican Sisters of the Order of Santa Catarina de Sena. The work is dedicated to the support of 40 young girls between the ages of three and twelve from broken homes.

Another Cecilia – Cissy Zino (née Bode) whose Swedish grandparents lived in Madeira – is a well known water colourist of Madeira's flora. Postcards of her work are available outside the English Church on Sundays and at the English Bookshop; originals are on the walls of Hotel Quinta Penha de França and Cliffe Bay Resort Hotel.

English Church

Now we go up Rua do Quebra Costas to the English Church also on the right. Fanny Burney Wood wrote of her first sight of it in 1838:

Today, Sunday, we went to the Protestant Church. A piece of ground surrounding the Chapel has been laid out as a garden. It looks singularly foreign for in England one always connects the sombre Yew or Cypress with a Church or Church-yard, and this is a blooming garden, in fact it is the gayest spot in Funchal from the profusion of

12. English Church by Emily Smith, 1842, courtesy of Quinta das Cruzes Museum

flowering shrubs and flowers with which it is filled; the scarlet and purple Salvias, introduced from England, are particularly luxuriant here.

Isabella de França describes her first visit to the church on 21 August 1853 in a typically lively way:

... the ladies go to Church, some in Cars drawn by oxen, some in Palanquims, or Hammocks, and some on horseback; many of the latter in white veils, silk mantillas or lace cloaks, and white or coloured muslin dresses, flounced above the knees; the flounces flying out from the saddle in the most ludicrous manner, for they do not trouble themselves to wear habits unless they intend to ride some distance. Some of the ladies had a large linen petticoat, which was put on like an apron hind part before, to preserve their dresses, which was slipped off at the Church door, and given in charge to the man who runs beside the horses, in his white trousers, blue jacket, and pointed cap, stuck on the top of his head, with its long tail standing upright. Altogether the scene was so truly ludicrous, and the trampling of the horses, the noise of the ox cars, the ringing or rather jingling of the bells round the necks of the oxen, the only bells we have, for we must not have Church bells, and the mingled cries of the drivers, the half English, half Portuguese phrases on all sides; made such a Babel of noises, that it was certainly the most un-Churchlike scene I had ever witnessed, and it took several Sundays before I could believe that I was not going to a Fair.

The pity is that Isabella's book, published in the twentieth century and beguilingly illustrated in colour by her own work, contains no painting of that scene, though the word picture probably suffices. On 3 March 1839, Fanny Burney Wood adds an equally delightful tailpiece to the English visiting their church on Sunday:

The Madeirans plant Creepers in pots on their Balconies and they have choice flowers standing on them to their adornment; — it makes the streets very cheerful and pretty. There is scarcely a house without a Balcony. The principal amusement of the Ladies, who rarely stir from home, is to lounge and chat over them, commenting on the passers-by. To such an extent is this habit carried that in Portuguese there is a word for it — a 'jannelleira' being 'a woman looking out of a window!'. On Sundays every window in the Carreira and the Streets leading from the English Chapel is filled with inquisitive black eyes all anxious to see the 'Inglezes' returning from Church.

As for the 1822 church itself, from the outside it is more like a theatre than a conventional place of worship, some suggest because the Protestants were not allowed to put up a church-like building. Today all is quiet and, at least during the week, deserted. The small garden is still charming, its main feature being a bronze bust of Philippa of Lancaster, Queen of Portugal. There is also a lending library in the grounds containing English-language books available to visitors as well as residents. (It is open on Friday and Saturday, 10.30 a.m. to 12.00 noon, and Sunday, 10.00 a.m. to 10.50 a.m.)

British Cemetery

Come back now to Rua da Carreira and continue along it to the end, to number 235, on the left. Here is the Protestant cemetery, now called the British Cemetery. The street door leading to its entrance appears locked and impregnable but you simply ring the bell and you will be let in (Monday–Friday 8.30 a.m. to 5.00 p.m.).

Nearly all visitors went to look at the Protestant cemetery, no matter how short their stay; Lady Brassey, for example, wrote on 19 July 1876:

Some of the inscriptions on the tombs are extremely touching and it is sad to see, as is almost always the case in places much resorted to by invalids, how large a proportion of those who lie buried here have been cut off in the very flower of their youth.

The most poignant description of the cemetery comes from **Emily Shore** (1819–1839). She arrived in Madeira at the end of 1838, aged 19. Her diary gives the impression that the family came for the health of her father, the Reverend Thomas Shore of Wadham College, Oxford, and, because of his refusal to toe the doctrinal line, their need to find somewhere cheaper to live than England. But it is obvious from what has already been quoted that her own health might benefit from the island's warmer climate.

As early as 24 December, she was taken, perhaps somewhat insensitively given what she wrote, to visit the cemetery – at that time divided into two: one for residents, the other for visitors. She recorded:

We first went into the former — a small gloomy spot, with straight walks and rows of cypress, enclosed with walls which are covered with half-effaced inscriptions; the stone coffin-shaped tombstones are over-grown with grass and straggling flowering-plants. Thence we went to the other burying-ground, which is much larger, and has all the appearance of a beautiful garden, with winding walks enclosed between the thickest hedges of geranium, four or five feet high, and so solid and massy that they appear quite different plants from the stunted and (comparatively) leafless specimens we see in England ... It was with a melancholy feeling that I gazed round this silent cemetery, where so many early blossoms, nipped by a colder climate, were mouldering away; so many, who had come too late to recover, and either perished here far away from all their kindred, or faded under the eyes of anxious friends, who had vainly hoped to see them revive again. I felt, too, as I looked at the crowded tombs, that my own might, not long hence be amongst them. 'And here shall I be laid at last,' I thought.

She wrote on Christmas day more cheerfully, 'Now that I am at last in this warm delightful climate, it is perhaps less unlikely that I shall see another.' But, by 13 January 1839, things were once more bleak as she wrote:

In Madeira I may possess content, and, indeed, as far as preservation from real misfortune and affliction goes, I ought to esteem myself happy; but all the *enjoyment* of happiness is gone, and cannot return ... There is nothing in Madeira which is dear to me; the land, the people, are new and unknown and strange ... The loss of health and strength has altogether deprived me of the active amusements, the rambles and observations of nature, in which I so much delighted, and has continually checked me in my studies, in which I delighted as much.

13. Portrait of Emily Shore, 1838, from *Journal of Emily Shore*

When, on 10 February, she was again feeling low, you may wonder if her diary is not all a tale of misery; but she was an intelligent young woman, well-educated, as her habits suggest and, in her best moments, eager to live. She wrote then:

I cannot describe the sadness and depression under which I suffered all the morning. I felt quite sick at heart, and languor of body added to the dejection of my mind. A gloomy hue seemed to tinge everything in this world. I thought it impossible I should ever be happy; I saw nothing for me to enjoy either in the present or future. I felt that I could willingly die, and almost wished that this long illness might indeed soon terminate in my release from earth. And yet when evening came, and I was again in the midst of our family circle, this feeling of melancholy left me, and I was surprised to find myself so reconciled to life.

Her diary continues until 1 April; then there is a gap until 18 May when she wrote: 'On the 4th of April I broke a blood vessel, and am now dying of consumption, in great suffering, and may not live many weeks. God be merciful to me a sinner.'

The last entry is on 27 May when she wrote, 'I feel weaker every morning, and I suppose am beginning to sink; still I can at times take up my pen. I have had my long back hair cut off. Dear papa wears a chain made from it. Mama will have one too.' She died in early June.

Her sister Louisa was with her from her arrival in Madeira; Arabella arrived not long before her death with their father. The family stayed on for some months afterwards living, according to Mary Phelps' diary, until August 1840 at Quinta das Angústias (see p. 62). Mary and Arabella were close friends of a sort. Mary noted not only that Arabella kept a beautifully written journal but that she wrote poetry, remarking 'I do believe she is a true poet but I somehow or other cannot fancy she will ever become celebrated as a true poet.' Later, however, Emily's sisters, following an example that was unable to reach fulfilment, became respected literary figures and advocates in the women's cause. And they edited versions of Emily's journal for publication. In one of their volumes of poems – *Elegies and Memorials* (1890) – Arabella writes of the death of both Emily and their younger brother; included are the lines:

> She lived on heights and knew not they were high.
> On fire, she knew not other souls were cold;
> She would have learnt it all, but was to die
> Ere yet her eaglet-wings could unfold
> For her true mates to search the world, and ask
> Her share in their appointed beauteous task.

The original volumes of Emily's journal had apparently disappeared but a new edition with an informative introduction was published in 1991. The editor, Barbara Timm Gates, tells how two volumes (of several) appeared for sale at auction when her new edition was ready for printing. She was able, at least, to sum up how Emily's sisters had edited her writing to convey the particular young woman they wished to present to the public.

I searched in vain for Emily's grave. It is not easy to find specific graves in the cemetery because of the changes that have occurred over time. Although there is a register kept on site (in the chapel), and you only have to ask to see it, it is incomplete. The cemetery is now divided into three sections – that furthest away, which I shall call (1); the one in the middle (2), followed by the most recent burials (3).

The first person to die and be buried in the Protestant cemetery (then called 'Factory Burial Ground'), newly permitted in 1765, was Mrs Shipcote, wife of a tavern-keeper, who died about 1770. But the register of deaths kept then at the British Consulate was carried out to sea in the floods of 1803 and that cemetery is now covered by the Largo do Visconde Ribeiro Real. In 1808, burials were started in a new piece of ground (1), at first for military personnel and their families during the Napoleonic Wars and British occupation. The ground rent was paid to the nuns of the Santa Clara Convent. That section is full of coffin shaped graves, as Emily Shore noted, marked only by numbers, together with graves such as those of the Reid, Wallas and Hinton families, and mural tablets around the square. New burials are beginning to be made there. In 1852 a new plot was acquired (2) which should include the Lowe memorial (see p. 23), but I could not find it, and does include a memorial to those whose remains were moved in 1890 – perhaps, among them, Emily Shore's. Several Cossart graves are here, as is Emma Penfold Stoddart's, though I could not find the rest of her family (see p. 129), and that of the Hon. Caroline Norton (see p. 104). In 1880, burials started in (3); the Blandy family has its own section here.

14. Portrait of Fanny Burney Wood, 1835, from Rolt, *A Great-Niece's Journals*

Fanny Burney Wood (b. 1812), her husband and one-year-old baby arrived in Madeira in September 1838 accompanied by two nieces who, since Fanny calls them wards, were perhaps orphaned – Margaret and Jane. Jane, aged 16, was dying of consumption, but there were many to die before her; on 13 December that year, her aunt wrote:

On the 7th inst. the thirteenth consumptive patient who has died since our arrival was buried in the Strangers' ground. The graves there are covered with geraniums, roses, and creeping plants, and many of the stones are invisible. All the associations of this spot are most melancholy, but there is none of the gloom of an English church-yard, and indeed upon first entering it is difficult to persuade oneself that it is not an uncommonly neat and well kept garden ... As I wandered round the burial ground I could not help thinking that if these stones could speak how touching would be many a history which they might record; of the young, the loved, the beautiful, who now sleep calmly beneath them!

All too soon, it was Jane's turn. On 17 February 1839, Fanny wrote of going in to see her on the 14th:

She told me that she had slept all night, 'most delightfully', expressed a desire for some more tea and thin bread and butter. After taking a little she shut her eyes, saying 'I must go to sleep,' but opened them to say, 'I cannot while you look at me': So Miss [Mrs?] Wardrop and I left her with her sister beside her. Then minutes later Margaret sent to beg me to return at once, which I instantly did. Alas! The pulse was scarcely perceptible. I seized her hand, and kissed her lips repeatedly, but grieved to see that she did not know me, for Death had indeed come.

Later that day, Fanny added:

The spot which I had chosen for her grave is under a large Cypress, in a quiet corner, in the prettiest part of the Churchyard. It is a rather singular coincidence, that the last time Jane walked out (the day before she was taken ill), she was to have gone with Mrs Temple to see the Burial Grounds, which she had not seen. They walked to the Chapel, but could not find the key, and so returned without entering; by which accident she never entered the place till she was carried to it in her coffin, the day three weeks that she was seized with the last phase of her malady.

And on 12 March she wrote:

I walked before Breakfast with Mr Smith to the Residents' Burial Ground, where is an old Orange Tree, the largest in Funchal, the trunk of which measures three and a half feet in circumference. In the Strangers' Cemetery I saw that the plants on dear little Jane's grave are beginning to take root. We watered and weeded them, and I made a sketch.

15. English Burial Ground by Lady Susan Harcourt, 1851, from Harcourt, *Sketches in Madeira,* 1851

Unfortunately, I could not find the orange tree and only one of Fanny Burney Wood's sketches of Madeira is used to illustrate her book (see p. 133). But Lady Susan Harcourt also sketched the cemetery and there, more than 150 years later, is a mural tablet with the inscription: 'Sacred to the memory of Jane Wood, youngest daughter of Colonel Thomas Wood CB Bengal Engineers, who died in this island February 14 1839 aged 16 years.' You will find it in (1) on the lefthand wall, behind the graves of the Reid family.

When you leave the cemetery, you may feel that you have done enough for one session. If so, stroll gently down Rua dos Aranhas where the Becco Chapel was (see p. 23), back to Avenida Arriaga.

Slavery

Next time, come back to Rua das Pretas. At its northern end it joins with Rua da Mouraria, forming a semicircle, both ends of which abut Rua da Carreira. A bit of a myth has been attached to these two streets, one which it is easy to buy into. Rua das Pretas can be translated as 'Black Women's Street' – that is, slave women – and Rua da Mouraria, 'Moorish Quarter'. It has been assumed that this area was a slave ghetto with all that implies – and I have walked up and down with that in mind. But the article *'Rua da Mouraria ou a Aventura Duma Palavra'* (Dr Ernesto Gonçalves, 1958), in Portuguese but with an English summary, has been brought to my attention. The author writes, ' "Rua da Mouraria" is merely a simple alteration of the original name: "Rua do Moradia" (Moradia's Street). "Moradia" was the nickname of a Madeiran nobleman of the sixteenth century, named João Rodrigues Cabral, a great-grandson of João Gonçalves Zarco, the First Captain of Funchal.'

He continues:

With regard to 'Rua das Pretas' (Street of the Negresses), the author of the present study disputes its origin and consequently its meaning: the name may have derived either from Negresses or from White women bearing the family name of 'Black' (Preto) who may have lived in the locality. As a matter of fact during the 15th and 16th centuries there were living in Funchal white people with the family name of 'Preto' (Black).

Slaves were brought in mainly to work on the sugar plantations and to act as domestic servants in town. But scholars of the island suggest that the numbers attached to each plantation were relatively small (compared with other Portuguese territories and America), and they were used as much to denote status as for work: to own a choir of women slaves gave kudos.

In the sixteenth century, **Dona Maria Gonçalves**, widow of António de Almeida and sugar plantation and mill owner, had slaves, though her sugar production was limited. **Dona Isabel de Abreu**, widow of João Rodrigues de Noronha, had two farms in the Lombada of Arco de Calheta and a personal 'Moorish girl'. Both women's existence in the records and their property suggest the distinctive status of upper class widows.

Slaves could be given, or buy, their freedom, and some such women, who might buy their freedom through pilfering from their owner, are recorded as fruit sellers or washerwomen. In 1615, of **Dona Branca's** 10 slaves, 2 were freed under her Will; one of them, named **Maria**, 'for being old and having served me very well and satisfying me totally.'

Some freed slaves even entered convents, for example, **Paulina**, slave of **Dona Apelonia Tavora**, and **Isabel**, belonging to **Dona Maria Câmara**. There are also parish records of the baptism of children of women slaves such as **Isabel** and **Gracia** of Funchal before the marriage of their mothers.

But not all slaves were owned by the Portuguese; and the story of Amelia finally brings to life the mere names I've managed so far to garner. Alice Leacock's husband, the British wine merchant John Leacock, wrote to America in 1763 to obtain, 'a good strong negro wench.' She had to be 'Reasonable, without faults, used to house works, that can cook well, Wash and Iron, between 20 and 30 years of age.' The following year he wrote, 'We have received the negro wench Amelia and are much obliged for your punctuality. As Amelia came ashore but yesterday we have not had an opportunity yet of knowing her disposition.'

Alice Leacock was soon to discover it; her husband wrote in November 1764, 'to acquaint you that the negro Wench you sent us does not at all answer the character given to her, and we fear you have been deceived in her, as to Cooking – she knows little or nothing, and is exceedingly Slow in what she does, and is likewise inclined to drink which last is a very bad Vice.' It cost £3 to ship her back.

More generally, there was some concern about the number of slaves, and the danger they might pose. They were, therefore, circumscribed in their movements, being required to live on their owner's property. Urban myths existed, as they have in many colonial societies, that the presence of slaves bred immorality, and that women, as well as men, might consort with their slaves. I have even heard it intimated that the reforming Prime Minister of Portugal, the Marquis de

Pombal, abolished slavery in 1761 because of these fears of slaves. The history of Madeira – where slavery existed legally until 1773 – was, until recently, hardly taught in schools, so slavery is not much talked about, though one informant told me that there is sometimes a consciousness of the slave past in physical appearance, as there is of the periods of Anglo-Saxon presence. Another informant told me she had always assumed that the black women of Rua das Pretas were nuns in black habits.

If you are still game to continue this itinerary without a break, go up Rua da Mouraria from Rua da Carreira until you reach the steep Calçada de Santa Clara. On the corner, with its entrance in Rua da Mouraria, is the Municipal Museum.

Municipal Museum

This was formerly the São Pedro Palace, then one of Mary Jane Wilson's first ventures in Madeira, St George's School and Pharmacy and where she founded her Order in 1884 (see p. 40). Its small aquatic collection bears no relation to either of its former uses, though it does also house municipal archives and you do get a feeling of the past simply by wandering around. It is not difficult to use your imagination about the buildings that survive in Calçada de Santa Clara.

Frederico de Freitas Museum

Next up the steep slope is the Frederico de Freitas Museum, sometimes known as the Casa da Calçada because it was owned, from the seventeenth century at least, by the Viscounts and Counts of Calçada. If you go downstairs and out, you will come across a perfect little garden where the women of the house were able to enjoy the view and some natural beauty in their seclusion.

In its eighteenth century reconstruction, which is what we mainly see today, it was rented from the 1940s by Dr Frederico Augusto de Cunha Freitas, a Funchal lawyer who was something of a traveller and collector. When he died in 1978, he left to the Regional Government his impressive collection of Madeiran artefacts; it bought the mansion from the Calçada family, converting it into a museum which opened in 1988.

It is an example of a historic house worth visiting for its association with families, as well as its contents from around the world. De Freitas was married to **Marieta Larica do Nascimento** who was not involved in his collecting but she did play an important role. Although their daughter **Manuela** died in her teens, and never lived in the house, it was fully-occupied – including his sister **Olga Teixeira** and her husband, and his mother, **Adelaide Augusta Cunha.** Dona Adelaide ruled the roost but it was Dona Marieta who made sure that everything ran smoothly, including frequent entertaining.

The museum is also especially interesting to us for its collection of mainly nineteenth century drawings and paintings by visitors to Madeira, among which are those of Isabella de França, together with her diary, which Dr de Freitas discovered in a London bookshop in 1938. These are not on display, mainly because watercolours are so vulnerable to light and atmosphere that they have to be protected. But I am assured by the Director, Dr Ana Margarida Camacho, that, should visitors have a good reason to see them, they may. And, from time to time, such treasures are exhibited.

This lack of permanent display is not as dire as it might seem for, in 1969, Isabella's diary, interspersed with her paintings, was published in Madeira not only in English – *Journal of a Visit to Madeira and Portugal 1853–1854* – but also in other languages. The book is not so difficult to come by on the internet. Available from the Museum is an edited version – *Vinte Ilustrações* (1998) – which includes the paintings and, in English, the text that goes with each one in Isabella's hand (with a translation in Portuguese). Either version is one of the nicest mementoes of Madeira because, as you will have gathered, Isabella's perception is not only unusual but warmly and ably conveyed. The diary itself, in one linen-bound ledger, is impeccably written, without any corrections and with picture numbers interspersed, and must, one deduces, have been prepared for publication. A venture that failed then.

Isabella de França (née Hurst) is unlike the other English visitors because of her marriage (aged 57) in London in 1852 to 50-year-old José Henrique de França. Although he was of Madeiran origin and a Portuguese citizen, his mercantile family had lived in England for some time and, through intermarriage, had become partly English. He did, however, own land in Madeira, had relatives there and had visited the island several times, though not since 1828–34. For all those reasons he was anxious, in August 1853, to take his wife (it was a first marriage for both) to see and be seen. She was kindly received and responded by loving everyone she met and appreciating all she saw. They were back in England by 23 June 1854; Isabella died in 1880, aged 85, José six years later.

The main part of José's family estates were in Estreito da Calheta (acquired by his ancestor who came from Poland in 1450) but that land was sold in 1864. We will go there in the itinerary 'From Funchal Westwards' (pp. 119–20). He also had lands just above Funchal, near Monte, and one day Isabella was taken to inspect those as well. We will go with her in the itinerary 'Flowers, Gardens and Walks' (pp. 114–15).

The Frederico de Freitas Museum has material from two other English women travellers – Sarah Bowdich and Lady Susan Harcourt. They have much in common, not only because their contribution was of drawings rather than a written record but also because both are airbrushed from accounts by their husbands.

Sarah Bowdich (c.1792–1865) is one of the earlier women travellers to leave a record. Although Sarah and Edward Bowdich had left Madeira in 1823, after a few months there, memory of them was still fresh when Fanny Burney Wood arrived in 1838. Her description conveys a quite specific image:

Mrs Phelps invited me to Breakfast to-day ... Mr Phelps told me several anecdotes of Bowdich, the African Traveller, who came here some years ago. He described him as a little, ill-made man (deformed, I think), very fond of talking and of dancing Quadrilles, while his wife, whom he in a great measure educated, was constantly studying and writing. Upon one occasion he happened to tell him that they had been reading his book upon Ashantee; he appeared charmed, and immediately launched forth upon the subject of his adventures, repeating the whole substances of his work! — he continued to discourse for three mortal hours, and fairly sent Dr Heinneken (a German Physician, practising on the Island), present as a visitor, fast asleep.

You might think from that anecdote that the Bowdiches, Edward at least, were of a certain age, but they were both only 32. Edward was, however, already a renowned Africanist and traveller and, since 1814, as the *Dictionary of National Biography* (*DNB*) suggests, Sarah's name 'is thenceforward so closely linked with his'.

Edward was born the son of a hat-maker and merchant and a Welshwoman from, it seems, the landed gentry. Sarah was born in Colchester, Essex, the daughter of John Eglington Wallis. When they married in 1813, Edward had just resolved to become a student at Oxford, but he soon left to take up a writership in the African Company, secured by an uncle. Sarah set out to follow him but discovered on her arrival in West Africa that he had left to return to Europe.

By 1815, they were back in Africa and he found himself promoted to deal with troubled relations with the Ashanti. With great deftness and courage he negotiated with the King and secured a treaty which the *DNB* says 'promoted peace to the British settlements on the Gold Coast'. Later he was to turn against the company; by then he was famous through his writing, particularly on the Ashanti. He and Sarah then spent four years in Paris where he extended his scientific knowledge and where the scientific community warmly received not only him but also 'his accomplished wife'. Three of his books had her illustrations.

In 1822, they set off again for Africa, via Madeira but, in Sierra Leone, as Edward continued his explorations, he caught a fever and died. In 1825, she edited, illustrated and had published his last work: *Excursions in Madeira and Porto Santo during the Autumn of 1823 while on his third voyage to Africa.*

The book is strange in that it is apparently written by him and as if she were not there, yet the signed illustrations show that she very much was and, as I have suggested when introducing to you the Curral das Freiras, some of the observations seem to be more likely hers than his. (Only the section on Porto Santo has his illustrations, suggesting that Sarah may not have been there). There is another quotation which sounds like Sarah in the section 'Flowers, Gardens and Walks' (see p. 124).

I hesitate to conclude from the anecdote that has him 'fond of talking and dancing quadrilles' and her 'constantly studying and writing' that her contribution to 'his' writing was substantial, but it would not be unprecedented and the *DNB* hints strongly that they were collaborators, though, in his lifetime, it was he who was renowned.

Sarah herself, in her preface to the (his) book and in her introduction to her tailpiece, is, it seems, deliberately ambiguous. In the preface she writes:

For the favourable reception of the first part of my book [i.e. his part], I feel little or no apprehension. The errors which may have crept in when correcting the press will justly be laid to my charge, and cannot deteriorate from its excellence. There, indeed, I have not presumed to make the slightest alteration not even by compressing the Supplement into the body of the work; feeling perfectly assured, that I had no right to deprive the public of one word, and that all attempts to improve would have been useless.

Sarah starts her own section:

I particularly lament that, contrary to his usual custom, his notes were very few and those so obscurely written, that even I who am so accustomed to decipher his memoranda can derive but little assistance from them: therefore, that I may not injure a reputation which stood so fair with the learned and the good, I must request my readers to consider me as responsible for every error.

It is worth noting that Sarah is one of those courageous and clever Victorian women who felt they had to introduce their work thus:

'Notwithstanding many important affairs of my own to attend to, and the few charms that politics possess for a female ...' She then proceeds to comment knowledgeably on politics.

The Bowdich book may well not be easy to find, either in an accessible library or at an affordable price (I saw it in the Bodleian Library, Oxford, having balked at buying it on the internet); but they do have a copy at the Frederico de Freitas Museum. It is certainly worth looking at, particularly if you are interested in fish – there are 57 of them, by Sarah. How she drew them it is interesting to speculate: did she after all go to Porto Santo? Did Edward bring 57 fish back from there for her to draw? Was there an aquarium in Funchal, or were there samples of the fish preserved there? Did she crib from an earlier publication? (An example of her drawing – of the Curral das Freiras – is on p. 7.)

On her husband's death, Sarah was left with three children and a living to make. She became well-known for her writing and illustrations of scientific books for children – the most popular being *The Freshwater Fishes of Great Britain* (1828). She married Robert Lee in 1829 and lived until she was 73.

Edward Vernon Harcourt wrote *A Sketch of Madeira: Containing Information for the Traveller or Invalid Visitor* (1851) as if his new wife, **Lady Susan Harcourt** (m. 1849, d. 1894), had not been there – she is not even in the acknowledgements – except that the book is illustrated with engravings from sketches by 'SVH'. Not only was Lady Susan with him but, unless she had been there earlier, so was his mother-in-law, for the book is dedicated 'To Harriet Countess of Sheffield this memorial of a beautiful island visited by her in 1848, is inscribed by her affectionate son-in-law.' There is, for those who follow footnotes, one which reads, 'See *Sketches in Madeira* by Lady SV Harcourt'; that leads you to a large folio of engravings made from her sketches. A copy of that is also in the Frederico de Freitas Museum, together with a couple of paintings attributed to her. These may be rough watercolours done on the spot, later redrawn with Susan's enviable precision. Or they may be copies by someone else of her work. Like the de França drawings, Susan Harcourt's work, having been on show for many years is, for reasons of conservation, now only exhibited from time to time. (You can see examples of her work from her published folio on pp. 45, 81 and 137.)

Both the Bowdich and Harcourt works are obviously treasures acquired by Frederico de Freitas in the same way as the de França diary and drawings. There are also a couple of framed prints by Emily Smith from *A Panoramic View of the City of Funchal* (1844) dedicated to the Dowager Queen Adelaide. I like to think that these views, one of which is reproduced in part on p. 58, encouraged Adelaide to go to Madeira. You will meet Emily more formally at the Quinta das Cruzes Museum (see p. 101).

Santa Clara Convent

The place most visited in the nineteenth century, and most written about, is our next port of call up the hill, the Santa Clara Convent, the foundation of which is detailed under 'Constança Rodrigues' (see p. 4). It was stripped bare by pirates in 1566 (see 'Curral das Freiras', p. 6) though some early tiles (*azulejos*) have recently been found on the chapel floor. Best of all for the modern visitor is that it remains the place most like it must have been 150 or so years ago. Its main attraction then was the nun **Maria Clementina** mentioned first by Henry Coleridge (nephew of the poet) in *Six Months in the West Indies* (1825). Because of the romantic image he conjured up, foreign women were drawn to the convent; everyone had to tell their Maria Clementina story.

The first sight of the convent itself comes from Maria Riddell in 1788 and it seems at that time the least interesting and most inaccessible visitor attraction; she wrote:

After Mass we visited the Convent of Santa Clara ... the votaries of her order at Madeira are not very numerous, the convent including but eighty nuns, and no novice having taken the veil for upwards of twenty years. This is a very strict order, for even the females of our party were not permitted within the grate. Indeed, the mansion appeared so gloomy and dismal, that I did not feel much inclination to pass its barrier. The nuns appeared extremely happy in our company, and entreated us to renew our visits often; but, on our taking leave of them, they assumed a very melancholy air, and candidly confessed how much they envied us our liberty.

Maria Clementina was born 15 years after that visit, c.1803, the youngest child of Morgado Pedro Aleixeira Agostinho Vasconcellos and **Ana Augusta de Ornellas**. The next of our travellers to visit the convent and the first woman to meet (and write about) Maria Clementina after Coleridge, was Fanny Burney Wood, on 24 December 1838; of the convent she wrote:

Being a Holiday, some of the Nuns were to be seen talking to their friends at the door, which was guarded on both sides by two formidable-looking ancient Religieuses, called the *Porters*, and hardy indeed would he or she have been, who could venture to force an entrance past these sour-visaged old ladies ... As I wished to purchase some Feather Flowers we were conducted up a flight of dark steep stairs into the 'Parlour', or room appropriated to those who wish to visit the Nuns, and talk with them behind the grating which separates the apartments from the rest of the Convent. This gloomy grating is double, and so close that it is difficult to distinguish the features of persons behind it, unless they sit at some distance from it. After a few minutes the inner shutters were unbarred and three Nuns appeared at the grating ... They desired us to choose some Feather Flowers from a circular wheel or box in the wall, which had just been turned round so as to display a selection of their work, by a person stationed within whose sole business it is to sit and superintend this machine.

Of the famous nun, Fanny added:

From the imperfect view I had of her through the curious iron bars it appears to me that her personal charms have been overrated, but she has a very pleasing voice and graceful elegant manners, which might have, I think, been always her chief attractions.

The day after Christmas was to be an open day, and Fanny set off once more; this time she wrote of her new friend and her guided tour:

Maria Clementina soon recognised me, and taking my hand, gently led me away from the rest of our party ...

My fair Cicerone led me into several of the Cells. Far from answering to my preconceived notions of such apartments, they were all pretty, gay, clean, ornamented little chambers. Some were tastefully decorated with flowers, both natural and artificial, fruits, specimens of needle-work, wax-work, and other ingenious manufactures, elegant little baskets filled with choice confectionery, china vases, French prints, and lithographs of Saints, Madonnas, and other scriptural subjects, which gave them rather the appearance of Boudoirs, than the Cells of a Nunnery.

In Maria Clementina's own cell, 'which was plainer than many', Fanny noticed several books, including Mme de Stael's *Corinne*. Fanny remarked that she had seen few books elsewhere and the nun explained that 'The Sisters had no taste for literature, and very little education; they did not employ their *minds* but their *fingers* in making a vast quantity of articles of fancy work.' As the tour progressed she learned that Maria Clementina was the 'Prima Donna among the Nuns, and leads the Singers at Mass.' Further on, Fanny learned that the Sisters, when they died, were buried under the stone in the Cloister. However, as her guide explained, there had been no deaths in the Convent for four years and the number of nuns, about sixty five, was unlikely to increase because the Queen (Maria da Gloria of Portugal; see pp. 24–7) had declared that there shall be no more Novices admitted. Maria Clementina also made it clear that not all the nuns were voluntary inmates, 'At least one half, if free to depart would immediately return to the world.'

Fanny obviously asked a great many questions (in French) – her journal entry on her visit is detailed and in depth, as this summing up suggests:

I perceived that her opinion of the mummery and pageantry of the Roman Catholic Church was not exalted, by the involuntary expression of her countenance. She said that many of the Nuns paid little heed to the prayers, and that she heard them talking during their performance in the most careless manner, upon totally indifferent topics. So much for the *piety* of these holy Sisters! She had been in the Convent eighteen years. I know not in what her charm consists exactly, but there is something indescribably interesting in her sweet voice and lady-like manners, which are rendered more striking by their contrast to those of the Sisterhood in general ... In her youth she may doubtless have been a very good-looking woman, though by no means so handsome as described. She is now thirty five years of age.

Back in Maria Clementina's cell, Fanny asked her if she herself had entered the convent voluntarily, and the Nun explained

... how, from her earliest childhood her Mother, a violent and bigoted woman ... had destined her for the conventual life, intending that she should enter a Nunnery at fifteen ... The bigoted parent consigned her pretty daughter to the Convent for life, painting the prospects in such glowing colours that the imagination of the young girl was impressed and she realised nothing of the tremendous sacrifice she was thus making ignorantly. The vow was irrevocably pronounced and the girl found herself cut off from the world for ever.

Fanny was 26 when she met 35-year-old Maria Clementina. That may be useful information knowing, as one does, how age and looks are assessed through the perceptions of a younger beholder. Emily Shore was only 19 when she met Maria Clementina; her visit to the convent was one of her first outings since arriving in Madeira and she wrote somewhat acerbically (and perhaps with added insight because of her own suffering) of 29 December 1838 (the day after Fanny Burney Wood's last visit):

No cell was so crowded as that of the well-known Maria Clementina, which seemed a general point of attraction. My curiosity to see this far-famed nun was now gratified. I saw her several times, and watched her narrowly to obtain an exact notion of her appearance. She seems now about seven and thirty, is far superior in personal attractions to the other nuns, and has the remains of some beauty; but how she could ever have risen into celebrity on that score, I cannot conceive ... her countenance was smiling and pleasant, but I thought not that of a mind at ease; there seemed lurking unhappiness beneath the surface, and there was a slight compression in her lips, which might have been affectation, but appeared to me to express a part of the same state of feeling. She really is, I believe, unhappy, and it is no wonder, for her former misconduct has given her a bad name in the convent, and the nuns avoid her; perhaps, too, they are a little jealous of her superior popularity.

Another 15 years were to pass before Isabella de França, then aged a sprightly 59, visited Maria Clementina, a mere 51. Isabella wrote more from the perspective of an insider of island Society and her report adds another element to Queen Maria da Gloria's times (see pp. 24–7); she also gives some hint of the 'misconduct' Emily mentions:

We had not been many days in Funchal, when we received a note from Maria Clementina, the celebrated Nun of Sta Clara, whose history has been so misrepresented in Coleridge *Six Months in the West Indies* ...

... The real history of this lady is that she is the Daughter of a noble family here, a Morgado house, and is very handsome, while her sisters are ugly. She was placed in the Convent of Sta Clara when very young and remained there until the year 1820, when the Constitution was proclaimed, and it was universally expected that all the Nuns would be set free, and the Convents abolished; at that time all strangers visited the Convent, but it is not now allowed to be shewn. A lieutenant of the Portuguese navy, whose ship was lying in the Roads, saw the beautiful Clementina, and they became engaged to be married as soon as the expected law should be passed; but in the meantime, the aspect of political affairs changed, the Constitution was overthrown in the year 1823 and all hope was for ever lost to poor Clementina; her lover sailed away, and here the romance ended, but she has ever since been the Lion of the English, in the Convent of Sta Clara; and all the Community make a kind of pet of her, and indulge her in many little fancies.

On 24 August 1853, Isabella finally meets the Lion and writes:

She presently entered, dressed in the most elegant and recherché style that the garb of a Nun will admit of. Her black dress was made open in front, and she wore a chemisette gathered into a narrow band round her throat, of muslin so fine and clear as to display the embroidered top of the slip, peeping under it; snow could not be whiter; and she held in her hand an embroidered handkerchief of the same muslin; she wore also a handsome amethyst ring on her finger, and her head dress was well calculated to set off her beautiful face and forehead; it was a black veil of some peculiarly transparent material, put over her finely formed shoulders; her beautiful hair was in bands, and was ornamented, not concealed, by a peculiar kind of Nun's cap, raised at the sides, and coming down over the forehead in a point, something in the style of the cap worn by Mary Queen of Scots, only that the point was so long and narrow, that it only concealed the parting of the hair in front, and left it at both sides open to view. Her dress was exactly the same as that of the other Nuns, only it was of much finer materials, and she made it becoming by the most scrupulous and studied attention to it.

Her carriage and manners are very elegant; she is now about fifty, but looks much younger, and the stately, though lady like manner in which she moves and speaks, are far more appropriate to the Court than the Cloister. Poor Maria Clementina! I took such a fancy to her, and felt so much interest for her. I shall never forget her! She was very cheerful, and chatted away very pleasantly, and laughed heartily, as we all did, when on taking leave, we tried to stretch our hands through the double grating, to shake hands with one another, and found that we could only just reach to join the tips of our fingers.

As for the other nuns, Isabella, with her acute powers of observation and sense of fun, noted that 'The back of the Convent looks over the part of the Town where we lived, and I was often amused to see the Nuns at their balconies and windows, with their veils thrown off for coolness, and pointing their telescopes in all directions to watch their neighbours.'

Taking the accounts of Maria Clementina, and the (twentieth century) remark by Isabella's editor, that when the famous nun was not available, other pleasing nuns were wheeled out in her place, it is difficult to resist seeing a public relations exercise in train: eager foreigners visiting the convent meant purchases of the handmade souvenirs. It is easy to see, too, why Maria Clementina may not have been entirely popular among her sisters.

Just before leaving Madeira in 1854, Isabella had occasion to add to what she had already written:

As I have said so much about the Nun, Maria Clementina, I must now record my last interview with her. On account of her health giving way, without any hope of recovery, she has been allowed to leave the Convent, and return to live with her Sisters, in Funchal, and is highly pleased at the compliment of being called upon, on her return to the world. Accordingly we made her a farewell visit, on the 23rd of May, but had I not remembered her voice, I should not have known her again as the beautiful Nun. She appeared better in health than when we saw her in the Convent, but the change to a secular dress, and that of the most unbecoming kind, had entirely ruined her appearance. The gravity of her manner was unchanged, and she expressed her greatest pleasure at seeing us again — but the beautiful vision is departed!

Lady Emmeline Stuart-Wortley who also visited Maria Clementina in 1854 must have done so just before she left the convent. Lady Emmeline was only three years younger than the nun when she observed that she had been 'a beautiful creature'; now 'she is no longer young (and I hope no longer miserable) but still are to be traced remains of her once brilliant beauty'.

Maria Clementina died in 1867 (aged 64). By 1881, when Ellen Taylor visited the convent, she was left with little to note save: 'The feather flowers, once so beautifully made in this convent, are now difficult to obtain unless ordered before hand.' The following year, **C. Alice Baker**, an American, was doing little more than passing through on board ship. Perhaps being held up in the harbour for some days because of quarantine regulations made her tetchy, or perhaps her experience explains why Ellen Taylor's description was so short; in any case, Alice Baker wrote of her visit to the convent:

Our carro driver seated us before a large double grating, a cruel separation between the nuns and the outer world, because neither hand nor lips can reach between to touch other hands and lips that are dear. The abbess, a big old woman of seventy, in a full robe of shiny black cambric, took her seat the other side of the grating. A tight fitting cap of black cambric came down in a point over her nose, arching over her eyes. She produced for sale to the strangers some ugly feather-flowers. Against our consciences we bought some, and we asked the lady superior how long she had been in the convent. Ever since she was eight years old, with the exception of two short intervals, when, on account of illness, she was allowed to go out. Sixty years of isolation from the world, with the mistaken idea that she was doing God's service with no better occupation towards her own development and that of others than the making of feather flowers.

Today, the convent is easy to spot: on the lefthand side going up, between the Frederico de Freitas and Quinta das Cruzes Museums, are big wooden double doors, with their brown paint peeling off. Above, and visible from a distance, is a quirky bell tower topped by a small, decorated dome. Florence Du Cane, whom you will meet more formally in 'Flowers, Gardens and Walks', wrote rather severely in 1909:

... One regrets the good old days when tiles, with their patterns in soft harmonious colourings, were used architecturally and let into walls in panels. There are still a few to be seen in the grounds of the Santa Clara Convent, and on the tower of the church, showing that in former days Funchal had probably more architectural beauty than it has today.

The nuns now run a kindergarten and primary school and are also prepared to take visitors round – the hours are shown by the doorbell which you should ring. Inside, you may see a group of tots in uniform sitting attentively in one of the cloisters. Maria Clementina has by no means been forgotten, though: you may be told of how a lover tried to climb over the wall to get to her – 'misconduct' indeed! The whole place reeks satisfactorily of the past. Opposite the convent is a building with a distinctive upper verandah; it is now government offices but it used to be the Santa Clara Hotel (see pp. 113–14).

Quinta das Cruzes Museum

Next on the left of the Calçada de Santa Clara is the museum that was also once a private house and, in an earlier manifestation, probably the site of the home of the discoverer of Madeira, Zarco, and his wife Constança Rodrigues. Zarco is buried in the Santa Clara Convent of which his granddaughter, Dona Isabel, was the first Abbess; Constança's burial place does not seem to be noted, though she apparently died in Madeira and two of her daughters are with their father's remains (see pp. 4–5).

The setting of the museum (established in the 1950s), overlooking the convent, and the fine garden scattered with pieces of historic masonry, are suitably evocative. The Zarco house was rebuilt in the seventeenth and eighteenth centuries, and added to in the nineteenth. The Genoan wine-shipping Lomelino family, who had arrived in the fifteenth century and prospered, took over the house in 1692. The chapel dates from their period.

Of the Lomelino family, the one of most interest to us is **Dona Luísa Susana Grande Freitas Lomelino**, better known as the writer Luzia (1875–1945). Her mother, **Dona Luísa Ana de Freitas Lomelino**, died giving birth to her in Portugal but, when she was six months old, her father – Captain Eduardo Dias Grande, later District Governor of Funchal – went to Madeira for his health and took his two daughters to live at Quinta das Cruzes, home of his late wife's parents. The garden at the quinta was 'an endless enchantment, a world ever new, with one discovery after another', Luzia wrote later.

Her father died of TB when she was nine, and she was sent back to her aunt in Portugal where she was educated and her interest in literature fostered. But, as a young woman, she returned to her grandparents. There she fell in love with a naval lieutenant, João de Vasconcelos de Couto Cardoso. They were married in 1896 in the São Pedro Church, still just down the road. She was 21 and she wrote later of how she was 'pushed, stunned, knowing nothing of life'. It was an unhappy marriage and they were divorced in 1911 after the Republic of 1910 allowed it. She described her situation in French, 'Little girl alone [*Seulette*], without companion or master.' She never remarried and died in Funchal at Quinta Carlos Alberto, Rua Jasmineiro (just past the Hospício).

Throughout her life, Luzia flitted back and forth between Madeira and Portugal, being a different person in each place. She wrote:

In Madeira I never talk politics; I don't know about the institutions; I don't recognise the seahorse, the civil revolutionary or the lady reactionary. One is quite unconcerned with the national problem and the future of the colonies ... Between your eyes and the ugly world you want that radiant veil of fantasy with which Eça [de Queirós, renowned Portuguese writer] dresses up the stark nakedness of truth ... Do you want to stay eternally young, eternally a little girl? Come to Madeira ... Since the servant who attends to us, the driver who drives our comfortable little carriage, the woman from Camacha who sells us flowers and the shop assistant who sells the embroideries, all call us *Menina* [Miss].

A friend wrote from Lisbon, 'When are you coming back? Don't get attached. You are from here, not from there.' Luzia replied, 'I already don't know where I'm from. Like some plants which put down roots in every land, wherever I arrive, I always consider that I've come to stay. I always feel part of it. I have my place at all the bridge tables. I belong to all the societies.' But in September 1919 she could write, 'Where will I be when the belladonnas open? Whence will the soft scent of the azaleas evoke my yearning?'

She published books such as *Cartas do Campo e da Cidade* (Letters from Town and Country, 1923) and *Cartas de Uma Vagabunda* (Letters of a Vagabond) but none appear to have been translated; nor were any available in print in Madeira. This may not be so surprising: I'm told that she had a tendency to use the lives, and scandals, of her acquaintances in her writing which may have soured her literary reputation. Her style may also seem a little overblown today.

I have found two extracts from Luzia's work in *A Madeira* (c.1958) an anthology of Madeiran writing compiled by João Cabral do Nascimento, in the British Library. Of the work of 37 writers, only three are women: besides Luzia, **Mariana Xavier da Silva** (1850?–?) and **Virginia de Castro e Almeida** (1874–1946). They do not seem to be well-known in Madeira. We will meet Luzia again in Jardim do Mar (p. 121).

16.   Luísa Grande ('Luzia') 1901, courtesy of Vicentes Photographic Museum

There is no sign of Luzia at Quinta das Cruzes now, though it was one of the scholars there, Ana Kohl Rodrigues, who brought her to my attention and made me a photocopy of the Portuguese biography *Luzia* (José Martins dos Santos, 1990). She and the Director, Dr Teresa Pais, and the Director of the Frederico de Freitas Museum are typical of modern Madeiran professional women, with opportunities and competence their grandmothers could not even dream of.

Although Quinta das Cruzes once belonged to the Lomelino family, most of the contents of the museum were donated by other families. Among them are drawings and watercolours of women visitors to, or foreign settlers in, Madeira. You may even be lucky and strike an exhibition for which other works have been borrowed. Once again, as at the Frederico de Freitas Museum, delicate watercolours are not on permanent display. The most interesting folio in the archives is 'Sketches by Emily Genevieve Smith'. A couple of her drawings were on the wall when we visited, and I have reproduced several others.

The identity of **Emily Smith** has been a bit of a mystery, now happily solved by one of my informants who, in England, came across the unpublished diary kept in Madeira from which I have already quoted. Emily arrived in Madeira in October 1841 with her husband, the Reverend Reginald Smith, vicar of West Stafford, near Dorchester. He had consumption and, like so many others, was recommended to spend time in the warm, supposedly dry air of Madeira. Emily Simpson (1816–1877), from Bath, had married her 'Reggie' (1809–1895), from a titled family in Dorset, in 1836, when she was 19 and he 26; they were to have eleven children and he was to outlive her, dying in his eighties. So the Madeira cure did sometimes work. Three of their children accompanied them to Madeira and she had another daughter there, in 1843. Her husband was often rather ill, so Emily's drawing and painting were undoubtedly therapeutic and she also gave singing lessons and quickly made friends. How long they were in Madeira is uncertain – not all Emily's diaries survive – but they left finally in the spring of 1843.

Among Emily's 356 drawings and watercolours are another 63 which are not signed by her. Six can be attributed to Miss White, one each to Miss Hayward and Miss Young, and three to Miss Penfold. The only clue I have found to **Ellen White** is that she probably had a sister called Mary who, in 1844, married John Garland; **Miss Hayward** must have been related to the British Vice-Consul, later Consul (1868–85) – Mary Phelps mentions several sisters in 1840: Ellen, Eliza, Fanny; and Miss Penfold's family appears in 'Flowers, Gardens and Walks' (see pp. 129–31). **Mary Young's** name has a historical resonance, explained vividly by Fanny Burney Wood on 22 October 1838:

Called on Miss Norton and Miss Young. ... The former of these ladies is the sister of Lord Grantley, the latter the daughter of Professor Young of Glasgow; they reside together, and having delicate health have chosen Madeira for their home. They have travelled much, and visited the Canaries together without any *chaperone*, and I believe intend publishing an account of their wanderings illustrated by drawings. They have made 150 beautiful sketches of the Fishes of the Island, which are to be engraved in a work upon the Natural History of Madeira, for which Mr Lowe, the clergyman of the English Chapel, has been for some years preparing materials. Miss Norton is a good-natured, eccentric person, who in virtue of her acknowledged oddity does the strangest things without anyone here being astonished, though in England folks would stare at some of her whims, and look scandalized, She is a first-rate horsewoman, and rides in cloth trousers, Wellington boots, and occasionally spurs! The contrast between these 'Aramintas' [unconventional literary women; see Maria Edgeworth's *Moral Tales*] is rather amusing to a stranger, Miss Young being as quiet and retiring as her friend is bustling and active, Miss Norton reminds me of a bottle of Mousseux or Sparkling Champagne which is well *up*.

Mary Young and **The Hon. Caroline Norton** (c.1798–1875) were already resident in Madeira by 1833. Richard Lowe, newly settled and then only acting chaplain of the English Church, wrote in a letter to William Hooker, his friend and fellow naturalist, that they 'are very delightful women, highly talented and accomplished. Miss Young is particularly so as an artist and you may be sure I was not slow to profit by her ready and unbounded liberality in drawing for me.'

In enclosing samples of Mary's plant drawings, Lowe hoped that Hooker might publish them in the *Botanical Magazine,* and he discreetly explained why he was trying to help her:

Miss Young's connections are so highly respectable and though her conduct under most trying circumstances has been (if you will take my word) most honourable in every way to her sex, she is obliged to have recourse to her talents for support: and to render this even more afflicting, there is reason to believe that the pittance allowed her would be withheld were this generally known to be the case.

It was Miss Norton who had explained this to Lowe and it was apparently Mary's father 'who has used her so ill'. Miss Norton hoped that by seeing his daughter's talent recognised in print, Professor Young might be brought round. Lowe, who was always rather prolix, went on to report that Miss Young

draws with great rapidity, has already a very competent knowledge of Botany, and is in every way so extraordinarily clever that she can, in short, do anything she likes to undertake. Her modesty and extreme liberality are only equal to her talents. I need only say further that she is prematurely gray-headed with affliction to interest you as deeply for herself as I am myself.

What one is to make of such circumlocution I leave you to guess. Hooker agreed to publish and offered Mary further commissions. Four of her drawings appeared in the *Botanical Magazine* in October 1834 for which she earned £20.

Those of Lowe's letters that survive do not mention Miss Young again; he refers some years later to a garden party given by Miss Norton. But both women must have remained close to him for *A History of the Fishes of Madeira* was published in parts between 1843 and 1860 under the authorship of R.T. Lowe 'with original figures from nature of all the species by the Hon C.E.C. Norton and M. Young'. To the specialist, this book may be seen as a companion to Sarah Bowdich's Porto Santo fishes – I made myself dizzy trying to compare them, to judge if the later work was entirely original. But whatever Lowe's reputation as a pastor (see pp. 20–3), that of his scholarly work is, it seems, untarnished and he spent even more years working as a naturalist in Madeira than he did in the Church.

As for Miss Norton, after a visit to the Santa Clara Convent on 26 December, Fanny Burney Wood added to her earlier word sketch:

Among the Nuns, Miss Norton, who visited them yesterday, is known as 'Lady Norton', and Maria [Clementina] told me that they were rather scandalised at her costume, which was her ordinary riding-dress; 'Elle est habillée exactement comme un Monsieur,' laughed Maria, and shrugged her shoulders expressively.

On 31 March 1839, Emily Shore described Easter celebrations and added, 'I understand, too, that at this time they are apt to caricature the English, dressing up people to represent the most remarkable. Last year the eccentric Miss Norton was thus represented, which gave her great offence.'

The Hon. Caroline Norton has led me (and a well-known library) quite a dance for she had almost the same initials (CEC) as her sister-in-law, the better known Caroline (CES) Norton (1808–1877) (whose bitter relations with her husband George, Lord Grantley's brother, and her campaign against his rights over their children and her property, influenced both the Infant Custody Bill of 1839 and the final provisions of the Divorce Act of 1857). Caroline Norton of Madeira, who published under her initials, is not mentioned in the standard reference works under the Grantley (title)/Norton (family name) entry, but I have now established some aspects of her identity beyond doubt.

First, there is her imposing grave in the British Cemetery in Funchal, with its inscription: 'The Honble Caroline Elizth Conyers Norton died 20 July 1875 aged 77 years ... In loving memory of a noble right minded and true hearted friend by Mrs Scott Gordon ...' Then there is her Will, which forms part of the historical record of her property, Quinta das Maravilhas. It was Miss Norton's vineyard there, you may remember, that was left unaffected by grapevine disease in the early 1850s (see p. 14). The picture of the house was painted in 1948, just before it was demolished by the current owner's parents and rebuilt a few yards further away. It was in less good condition than the artist's licence suggests. The new house is privately owned and is neither visible nor visitable.

In the Will, which Caroline drew up with a lawyer in Portuguese, with which she was fully conversant, just before her death, she left the quinta and all its contents to Elizabeth Scott Gordon, 'married and who lives in my company; and I also leave her some land which I possess at Sitio do Ribeiro Seco of this same village'. She made the strict proviso 'that items bequeathed her in no way should merge with those of her husband ... as it is she whom I wish to benefit in view of the good company she has kept me, her care in my illness and our reciprocal friendship'. She disposed of her English assets separately.

17.   Quinta das Maravilhas by Max Romer, 1948, courtesy of Jeremy and Emília Zino

And what had happened to Mary Young? Caroline makes clear that she was already dead, and buried in the Old Cemetery – in a plot which Caroline had owned. I could not find Mary's grave, nor a record in the register.

A footnote to this story has become unavoidable. That a woman called The Hon. Caroline Elizabeth Conyers Norton existed in Madeira is irrefutable but that she was a sister of Lord Grantley is more complicated. While there is apparently no Grantley sister called Caroline in the genealogical records such as *Burke's Peerage*, there is one called Augusta Anne Norton (and one called Grace Conyers Charlotte). In biographies of the famous Caroline Norton, recorded physical and behavioural descriptions of Augusta correspond with those of Madeira Caroline. Since Burke's suggests that Augusta married in 1846 and had children, which does not accord with the facts of Madeira Caroline, I can only suggest there may have been two Norton sisters who (like the two Carolines) have been confused. As for the record, the family may have expunged Caroline for reasons which one can only surmise. Neither the Grantley family today, nor the most recent biographer of Caroline Norton, knows of Madeira Caroline, nor can they explain the mystery.

18. Convent of the Incarnation by Mary Young, 1843, courtesy of Quinta das Cruzes Museum

If you can accept for the moment that Augusta and Caroline Elizabeth Conyers have been confused, an added twist is as strange, for the hostility between the two Caroline sisters-in-law in biographies is marked. Did novelist, poet and tract writer Caroline visit her sister-in-law Caroline in Madeira? If not, she must at least have taken account of her residency there for, in 1835, she published the novel *A Woman's Reward* which starts off on the island. A merchant father is dying of consumption in Madeira; his wife is already dead; the setting is quite detailed. But by page 38 the 15-year-old heroine, Mary Dupré, and her impossible brother Lionel, now orphaned, have left for England.

There is no evidence that 'an account of their wanderings illustrated by drawings' was ever published by the two women, but an idea of Mary Young's talent can be gleaned by the drawing of 'the Convent of the Incarnation'. Quite apart from their artistic endeavours, their lifestyle and Caroline's Will suggest that, even in Victorian times, Madeira was a place where a woman could be herself more easily than in England. And, for mid-nineteenth century novelists, Madeira was a useful, faintly exotic, off-stage setting: the uncle who left Jane Eyre his fortune made it there.

Municipal Square (Funchal)
Eastwards and Southwards

Rua de João Tavira, Municipal Square, Museum of Sacred Art, Bom
Jesus Convent, Houses of Pleasure, Institute of Embroidery, Mary
Jane Wilson Museum, Rua do Carmo and Reid's Hotels, Largo
do Phelps

Rua de João Tavira

The easiest place to start this itinerary, too, is the Cathedral (in Avenida
Arriaga). This time, take the immediate road north, Rua de João
Tavira, which brings you into Rua Câmara Pestana, a continuation
of Rua da Carreira. A right turn leads you into the Municipal Square
(Praça do Municipio).

The Phelps had one of their town houses in Rua de João Tavira
and Fanny Burney Wood and her family, including her consumptive
niece, stayed there briefly on their arrival in September 1838, before
moving nearby to Mrs Wardrop's place.

Opposite the Phelps' house is where the sickly Emily Shore and her
family stayed. Strangely, although they were living in the same area
at the same time, 19-year-old Emily does not mention 16-year-old
Jane Wood, and Jane's aunt does not mention Emily. Mary Phelps,
however, mentions both families, though she seems to have been
closer to the Shores, particularly after Emily's death. She didn't care
much for Mrs Wood. There do seem to have been several circles of
acquaintance often, as we have seen, depending on their religious
affiliation. Emily wrote of her first impression on approaching their
accommodation from the ship on 21 December 1838:

We began scrambling up the beach, and I was actually able to walk all the way to
the Houghtons' house. It is not above five minutes' distance from the shore, but the
streets are steep and fatiguing. We passed through the Public Walk, which is planted
with trees, and by the gates of the cathedral. In a very narrow street we stopped at
the door of Messrs Houghton and Burnett. We entered a small dark stone hall, which

contained some empty casks, and a flight of very prison-like stone stairs. The rest of the party walked up first, and two Portuguese men-servants carried me up in a chair, so that I was landed without fatigue in a very handsome suite of rooms ...

When we came to the dining-room they threw open the Venetian blinds, and with delighted astonishment we looked down on a garden crowded with the richest green foliage, which, amidst the blaze of Madeira sunlight in December, looked as refreshing as a cool wood in an English July. I do not think any garden was ever so charming in my eyes, it was so surprising and unexpected.

Although this street is now a pedestrian precinct, and there is a shopping centre on your left, many old houses remain and the whole effect is pleasantly historical. It is not clear, however, which house belonged to whom.

Municipal Square

Turn now into the charming square round which cluster Funchal's distinctive Municipal buildings (mostly former mansions) – well worth seeing but not much about women. A statue of Leda and the Swan (1880) adorns the courtyard of the Town Hall (straight ahead of you), once the eighteenth century mansion of the Count of Carvalhal (see 'Quinta do Palheiro', pp. 154–6).

Museum of Sacred Art

On the right of the square, the Museum of Sacred Art contains an unexpected collection of Flemish art (found by chance throughout the island) including the triptych of St James and St Philip, the side panels of which show the family of the grandson of Constança Rodrigues, Simon Gonçalves da Câmara, who commissioned the painting. The sixteenth century 'Adoration of the Magi' by Grão Vasco was given to the Chapel of the Magi in Machico by its founder Branca Teixeira, wife of Tristão Vaz who, with Zarco, discovered Madeira (Machico fell within his purlieu as joint-Governor). The two side panels of the triptych of the 'Descent from the Cross' may show the commissioners of the painting, Simon Acciaiuoli and his wife **Maria**

Pimental, also known as **Mary Drummond**. (John Drummond, brother of Annabella, queen of Robert III of Scotland, had taken refuge in Madeira in 1425 and married **Branca Affonso** of Santa Cruz; Maria's mother was a Drummond.) If the painting came from a different church, the donors were Jorge Lomelino and his wife. 'Santa Maria Madalena' was commissioned by **Isabel Lopes**, widow of João Rodrigues, according to her Will of 1524. There are also examples of sixteenth and seventeenth century vestments embroidered by the nuns of Santa Clara.

Bom Jesus Convent

Beyond the Muncipal Square, you cross two main roads either side of the Ribeira de Santa Luzia and come to Rua do Bom Jesus. On the corner of that and the northern part of Rua da Conceição is a seventeenth century women's religious establishment, the Bom Jesus, now a lay convent (*residencia leiga*). Mrs Wardrop's place, whence Fanny Burney Wood and her family moved in November 1838, was nearby. Fanny described how 'the turret of our house looks down upon the Convent of the Bon Jezus'. What she wrote next outdoes Isabella de França's account of the goings on at the Santa Clara:

We are often entertained by watching through the Telescope up there ... a Flirtation active and continuous carried on between one of the inmates of the Convent (Portuguese gentlemen on leaving home for any length of time often place their wives or daughters at the Convent to be kept out of mischief) and a young man who resides in the next house to us. Both the swain and his 'inamorata' are provided with telescopes, and besides holding these long conversations upon their fingers, they have a variety of telegraphic signs with handkerchiefs, etc., only understood by themselves. They sometimes spend an hour or two thus. Flirtations of this kind are very common.

There is a house on the opposite side of the little side street that you feel sure was Fanny's lookout.

This lay retreat was not secular in 1910; indeed, it was here that Mary Jane Wilson was detained when the Revolution was proclaimed (see pp. 58–9). She had taken it over in 1906 because the Bishop was concerned about how it was being run, and the attitude of the inmates – obviously a long term problem. She found herself embroiled in dissent both internally and from the republican newspaper *O Pópulo* (*The People*). The Republic itself determined the outcome.

Houses of Pleasure

Rua do Bom Jesus leads into Rua de João de Deus. Here, until quite recently, you could still see examples of *casas de prazeres* – 'houses of pleasure'. These were not quite as they sound. When Catherine of Braganza married Charles II (see p. 10), she took with her the Portuguese custom of afternoon tea. The *casas*, built on the garden walls of quintas, were simple and airy summer houses, with trellis-work or shutters and traditionally decorated with Madeiran embroidery and English chintz, where this five o'clock ritual took place. Continue along the street eastwards to the end, resisting the temptation to turn down Rua Mary Jane Wilson on your right towards the end.

Institute of Embroidery

Turn right at the end of Rua de João de Deus. You are now in Rua do Visconde da Anadia and there on your right is your landmark, the statue of the *bordadeiras*, set back slightly from the road. Number 44, a few yards further down is the Institute of Embroidery, Tapestry and Handicrafts (Instituto do Bordado, Tapeçarias e Artesanato da Madeira – IBTAM). As you ascend the stairs, you are faced with a huge tapestry of scenes of Madeira, done in Gobelin stitch, which was started in 1959 by 16 schoolgirls and finished three years later. Upstairs is a fascinating museum containing displays of fine lace and embroidery, mostly done between 1880 and 1915. Strangely, perhaps, Bella Phelps' name is not mentioned (see pp. 28–32). In the first room there is a print of Emily Smith's panorama of Funchal (see p. 58).

Mary Jane Wilson Museum

Turn back now into Rua de João de Deus and left into the narrow Rua Mary Jane Wilson. I knew that this street existed – it is marked on some maps. And gradually I discovered, from biographical entries in Portuguese on the internet, what happened to Sister Wilson following her return to Madeira. In October 1916 she was asked by the Bishop to set up a school in the dilapidated Convent of São Bernadino at Câmara de Lobos for children who would later attend the diocesan seminary. She came out of semi-retirement in Santo da Serra and set to with a will, but the strain was too much: by 18 October she was dead. Though she was buried in Câmara de Lobos, in 1939 her remains were transferred to the Chapel of Quinta das Rosas in Rua do Carmo, Funchal, the Mother House of the Order she had founded.

I did not know that her Order was still going strong, nor that the memory of Sister Wilson was very much alive; indeed, efforts are in train that may lead eventually to her beatification. A chance sighting of a nun in a habit emptying a bucket into a drain outside a blank looking building in the street that bears her name led to the discovery inside of the chapel to which her remains were taken and the Núcleo Museológico Mary Jane Wilson, opened in April 2003.

The museum is formally and easily approached at 61 Rua do Carmo (turn left at the bottom of Rua Mary Jane Wilson). We were taken to the chapel and then introduced to the elegantly devised museum most kindly by Sister Kirila, who had in earlier years opened a House in London, and Sister Edith. They are retired from teaching – and the Mother House is primarily a refuge for retired members of the Order – but devoted to the memory of their founder in the form of a museum that is well worth a visit. As well as a trail of spacious rooms, fitted with blond wood, illustrating Mary Jane Wilson's life and work, there is a wall of her drawings, done during her earlier, more secular life. And on another wall is a large painting of Christ, from the chapel at Santa Cruz, painted by her. Easily missed is a lock of her baby hair in her mother's locket. In the front of the museum are any number of relevant publications and cards. The route from there to the chapel is lined with the climbing roses from which the quinta takes its name (see also pp. 39–43, 46–50, 58 and 116).

Rua do Carmo and Reid's Hotels

Lady Emmeline Stuart-Wortley says that in 1851 she stayed in an apartment in 'Mr Miles's hotel' on, as she described it, the 'principal street' – which others agree was the Rua da Carreira. Mrs Henry Cust, who wrote *Wanderers: Episodes from the Travels of Lady Emmeline Stuart-Wortley and Her Daughter Victoria 1849–1855* (1927) says that her grandmother and mother stayed at Mr Miles' Hotel in 'The Rua Carreira'. Ellen Taylor wrote 30 years later that 'The Carmo Hotel better known as Miles Hotel, has for many years been one of the chief and best managed hotels and is comfortable in every respect (proprietor Mr Reid).' But Ellen's map, not surprisingly, places the Carmo or Miles Hotel on the Rua do Carmo, to the right of the Carmo Church. William Reid the younger managed the hotel and when he married in 1892 his place was taken by Mrs Edith Richards who was some years later to become his brother Alfred's second wife.

The founder of the Reid dynasty, William George, came to Madeira from Scotland in 1836 as a 14-year-old. Beginning to prosper, in 1847 he spotted a gap in the market and started letting rooms in Funchal's quintas to visitors during the winter months. Such a visitor was the Marchioness Camden who rented Quinta de Santa Luzia for two years, bringing with her 28-year-old **Margaret Dewey** (c.1819–1875) as her companion. Reid was immediately smitten and married Margaret that year; they were to have twelve children. Together they saw another gap and bought Quinta das Fontes which they turned into a hotel (The Royal Edinburgh, now the Marina shopping centre near the waterfront, see p. 60). By the 1880s, they owned several hotels in Funchal. Ellen Taylor stayed at the Santa Clara Hotel and also tells us that Reid was the proprietor of Deutsches Hotel in Rua das Hortas. Of the Santa Clara – opposite the convent – she wrote: 'This hotel is the hotel *par excellence* – spacious, well-ventilated, and very comfortable, above the town and yet sufficiently near to be very convenient.' The original hotel is now government offices but there is still a Residencial Santa Clara nearby (see p. 97).

Clara Reid (1868–1924, née Lawson) and her husband Alfred, of the second generation, managed the Santa Clara Hotel. Her daughter Blanche tells how the music hall star **Marie Lloyd** (1870–1922) came to stay. On being shown to her room, she was horrified to see that 'the cretonne had a design of peacock's feathers. She refused to sleep there – she would have bad luck, she would forget her lines, and goodness knows what else.' Clara continued active in the hotel almost until Blanche's birth.

Blanche Reid (1891–1977), was always known as **Tommy** because she was supposed to be a boy. In the (unpublished) record she made of the Reid family in Madeira towards the end of her life, she describes how the Hotel Carmo stood in a walled garden dominated by an enormous camphor tree and so sheltered that sub-tropical plants flourished. Several guests were from Africa and one turned up with some lion cubs which he was taking to London Zoo. His departure date was so delayed that the cubs increased in size and strength. 'One morning,' Tommy writes,

the diminutive figure of my mother (she was under five feet) was crossing the tennis-court when the young lions broke out, bounding round her in high spirits as she lay on the ground. The horrified owner rushed to her rescue, full of admiration for her presence of mind and self-control in lying, as she did, absolutely motionless.

Links between West Africa and Madeira were interesting, and we are not talking only about slavery. In 1849, Captain Forbes of HMS *Bonetta*, trying to persuade King Gezo of Dahomey to give up his part in the trade, was given a young girl who became known as **Sarah Forbes Bonetta**, a celebrity in England and Queen Victoria's goddaughter. She married the Sierra Leonean merchant James Davies in 1862 and returned with him to Africa. But, when she became ill in 1880, she travelled to Madeira in the hope of regaining her health, and died there.

There is no longer a Hotel Carmo, but walk westwards from the Mary Jane Wilson Museum towards the Largo do Phelps. Just before you reach it, and before the Carmo Church, on your right is a large modern block with *Edifício do Carmo* in arty lettering on the side. This is the site. The better-known Reid's Hotel is described in the 'Waterfront' itinerary (see pp. 67–8), and the family's quinta and their life there is described in 'Flowers, Gardens and Walks' (see pp. 149–53).

As for Lady Emmeline, we will simply have to imagine the doughty widow, eyes glinting, parading with her daughter Victoria down both Rua do Carmo *and* Rua da Carreira.

Largo do Phelps

Your imagination has to work in overdrive in Rua do Carmo but, as you reach Largo do Phelps, you get encouragement. Although there is no sign now of the Phelps house and business, let alone Elizabeth, Bella or Mary Phelps, the square is bustling and bijou – and there are some nice enough shopping streets leading off which include embroidery establishments. It is a good enough note on which to end this itinerary.

From Funchal Westwards

Câmara de Lobos, Ribeira Brava, Paúl da Serra, Rabaçal, Estreito da Calheta, Jardim do Mar

The womanly point of this itinerary is to end up where Isabella de França visited her husband's old family property and where Dona Guiomar and Luzia also have a connection.

Câmara de Lobos

Driving westwards out of Funchal, you come, about eight miles out, to Câmara de Lobos. This is where Zarco first set up camp in 1425 and from where he initially governed his part of Madeira. Given the date of the Caterina Chapel, Constança must have been with him. It is also where Mary Jane Wilson died, in the Convent of São Bernadino (see p. 112). Leaving the fishing village and climbing upwards, there is a road leading sharply down into the valley; the convent, now simply a church, is down there. The original was founded by **Isabel Correia** and her husband in the sixteenth century and restored in the eighteenth and nineteenth centuries. The day of our visit we had to get back for our driver's next appointment, with a fair drive ahead of us, and that road is 'no entry'. So we pushed onwards as I struggled to look back and catch a glimpse. Leaving the village the intensity of cultivation, including vineyards, begins to strike you. Remember that Dona Guiomar had vineyards here in the eighteenth century.

Ribeira Brava

You enter the valley of Ribeira Brava. Our driver, Martinho, who was a marvellous informant during both our visits to Madeira, was born towards the top of one of those peaks and claims that the whole vista is more impressive than the Curral das Freiras. The road now approaching the top from behind was not there in his mother's day. When I asked if women in the countryside still do embroidery, he described for me a day in the life of real country women in the mountains, one that is still largely unchanged, and hard. As well as looking after the family, women do agricutural work. If it is too cold and wet that morning, they might do an hour or two of embroidery to supplement the family income. They cut the long grass and carry it on their heads to feed the animals. After making the lunch, they might do some more embroidery, depending on the weather, and then continue their other labours. In the wicker weaving areas, a similar routine is followed – women work the willow at home and then take it to the factory to be paid. This whole drive is an eye-opener to a different sort of Madeira from that previously seen, with its intricately cultivated, narrow terraces latched precariously onto mountain sides. But you have to go further inland, away from the developing coastal belt where the climate is mild, to see real mountain life in the raw.

Paúl da Serra

You can drive all the way to Jardim do Mar by a coastal road cut into the mountain side, rising and falling into valleys and up and out again. We came back that way. On the outward journey, we turned right at Ribeira Brava, up into the mountains and then turned left onto Paúl da Serra (Moor on the Mountain). I wanted to see that because much of Ann Bridge's spy novel *The Malady in Madeira* (1969) is set there. It is by no means her best – those set in Peking are rather good; it is more something to read when befuddled by sun and wine, but it is about the only English-language novel set in Madeira that I feel able to recommend.

Now, having been to that wide, deserted plateau, where the mist swirls as often as not, I appreciate Ann's setting more. When she decided to use the plateau, it was the home of sheep grazing, the crux of the story. Fanny Burney Wood and her niece Margaret were taken there in a party on a tour of this part of the island in April 1839; she wrote of the Paúl da Serra:

When we had rested we proceeded at a rapid pace across the level of 'the Paul,' which is covered with Broom, Heath and Whortleberry, about the height of a man.

The Serra is celebrated for a small breed of strong, active Ponys, of which we saw many grazing; also Oxen, and a few black Sheep and Lambs.

How it has changed! Because those animals over the years have eaten their fill, there is now little vegetation; erosion threatens and all animals are banned. It is a spooky place on the right day. If you walk there though, the smell of wild thyme lifts the spirits.

Rabaçal

When you reach the far edge of Paúl da Serra, there is a road winding down on your right into the valley of Rabaçal. It was closed because of inclement weather the day we passed but it is apparently a good place for walking, as your walking books will detail, and there is a government rest-house to welcome you.

It must be at the point where the road starts down that Isabella de França descended in 1854 on an outing from Estreito da Calheta and wrote:

We now began the descent to the Rabaçal, which is by a succession of zigzags, forming what is called a road, cut through a forest of laurel, myrtle, and other evergreens, growing so thickly together, that the whole forest seemed one tangled mass of leaves. The descent is perfectly frightful; the rock through which it is cut, is so steep, both above and below, and the road so narrow, that every time the rede [hammock] passes one of the many turnings, you hang over the precipice without seeing a particle of the road itself, and are literally suspended over the abyss beneath, while the rede is turned!

And one of her inimitable paintings, with her and José in hammocks, illustrates that passage. Fanny Burney Wood felt much the same and wrote:

We reached the edge of a wide thickly-wooded ravine. Here all excepting myself alighted, the path down to the bed of the river being far too narrow and precipitous for horses. We descended down a frightfully steep and bad path where it was all but impossible to pass the peasants whom we encountered with loads of Brushwood and Broom ... I entreated my Bearers to allow me to walk, for I was really afraid of the miserably bad road if I continued to be carried in the Hammock, but the men seemed to consider it a point of honour to carry me as long as possible, and would not hear of my alighting.

But it was all worth it:

The whole of this Janella (Window) Ravine is exceedingly lovely, richly covered with Heath, Broom, Bilberry, and Sweet Bay, interspersed with Forest Trees, down to the very bed of the river, over which at the spot where we crossed grow some magnificent old Til Trees ... By jumping from rock to rock we crossed the Ribeira and ascended the opposite side of the Valley for some distance, till at last I left my Hammock and walked onwards with the rest of the party to the 'Fontes,' or 'Aguas de Rabaçal,' which is a collection of springs of water falling from a kind of large natural tank or reservoir in the rock, over a cliff 250 feet high, through fissures in the rock, into the Ribeira below.

Lady Brassey was taken on a similar trip in 1883 when the weather was her main concern; they were soaked to the skin hardly had they moved. She wrote:

I never thought of danger at the time, there was so much to distract my attention, though I suppose it was really a somewhat hazardous expedition; but the beauty of the scenery atoned for all the peril incurred. The Twenty-five Fountains ... consist in reality of one high waterfall, tumbling over a perpendicular precipice, and in places almost hidden by the luxuriant growth of trees and other ferns, amid which little water-spouts spurt and jet out in every direction. I counted thirty instead of twenty-five 'fountains'; and there were numberless small ones besides ... What would it have been, I wondered, on a warm, bright, sunny day?

Women travellers were so much more hardy in the nineteenth century!

Estreito da Calheta

The road to your left as you leave the Paúl da Serra is the way to Estreito da Calheta and the de França quinta (see pp. 85–6). You pass small farmsteads and women walking with bundles of vegetation on their heads.

The editor of Isabella's journal told us in 1969 that the house still stood and was called Quinta da Varanda, of which only a small part was then habitable. In her journal, Isabella describes the whole journey there and back by boat in intricate detail as well as their time in the area. It is possible to go to Calheta, the village below Estreito da Calheta, by boat today, but only in the summer which starts officially at the end of April. Ask for details at the Marina in Funchal (see p. 58). But, of course, if you do that, you will need transport up the hill. Isabella and José should have been met by the bailiff of their quinta but messages had gone adrift; they had to clamber up.

Even in 1853, long before the property was sold, they were camping in the house and she writes:

But in the midst of all this apparent splendour, it was melancholy to see it all going to ruin; the floors trembling as we walked over them, the crimson velvet faded to a light brown, the paint and gilding black and tarnished, & the beautiful ornamental locks all out of order. I could have cried to see so beautiful a place so gone to decay, and wished I had had thousands to spend in restoring it!

This is what I had set us to find in April 2004!

Estreito da Calheta is a rather different place now, even to 1969. Development has raced ahead: a myriad villas overlook the sea far below; there are plenty of cars and a new trunk road is being bulldozed right through. No one had heard of Quinta da Varanda. Martinho was getting late for his appointment – 'We must turn back,' I pronounced generously. We rounded a bend, and there it was, perched on the hillside, already more than half dismantled – verandah gone, hardly more than a shell, with windowless holes looking blindly at the lovely view. But we all knew that we had reached our goal. There was no time to do more than take photographs from the bend in the road and stop at a wayside business in the lee of the quinta to ask if that house was known as Quinta da Varanda. It was.

Back in Funchal, we did some less subjective checking, not only with someone who comes from the area. It transpires that a scholar has recently inspected the quinta and noted the de França coat of arms. But the house looks due for demolition. I like to think it will be saved, if only to give you a real purpose for this fascinating drive.

Almost more interesting than Isabella's description of her stay at the quinta was her passing observation of **Dona Joana de Albuquerque**, wife of Francisco Estanislao de França (m.1835), a cousin who lived nearby. When a young girl was brought to her with a badly cut head the 'Surgeon of the Parish … sewed up the wound with her own hands, and applied the proper remedies'. This incident opens a small window onto the life of upper class women in the countryside as opposed to town. And it would be good to know more about 'proper remedies', perhaps herbs collected in the mountains, a lore passed on down the generations of women.

Jardim do Mar

We did not drive on to Jardim do Mar; fortunately, given our time restraints, I did not then know about Dona Guiomar or Luzia. Driving back along the coast road, you will pass through Calheta, Arco da Calheta and Madalena do Mar – all this area is intensively cultivated on breathtaking cliff-side terraces, as well as in valleys. Dona Guiomar had vineyards in each of these localities, as well as Jardim do Mar – growing Malvasia grapes and producing wines of rarity and profitability. Whether or not she ever visited her vineyards there, I don't know; I wouldn't put it past her (see pp. 11–13).

A hundred years later, the writer Luzia found herself in Jardim do Mar during an unhappy period of her marriage – her diary describes bitter quarrels and a despotic, uncaring husband. She wrote:

During those years when I lived in Madeira, I spent three winter months in a little fishing village, called Jardim do Mar, which was then more wild and primitive. There I lived in a sad mansion, an old manor house of my husband's, beside a chapel, where many of his ancestors were buried. We had several weeks of gales, when we were cut off like Robinson Crusoe. The hail lashed the glass of the windows and there was such an enormous din at night that we could not sleep … Then one day, the wonderful day of the miracle, when everything was transformed. The horror, the disgust, turned to enjoyment, to pleasure. The hateful months became the best of the year. I can't say precisely what worked the miracle. Love filled the bushes with roses, making an oasis in the desert.

This was the Quinta da Piedade, a summer home of the Couto Cardosos; it still belongs to the family. Unfortunately, it is not quite the tranquil place it once was; at the time of writing, I'm told that a public car park is being built behind. The present owners hope that one day they will be able to enjoy it fully again.

Flowers, Gardens and Walks

Florence and Ella Du Cane, Quinta da Achada, Quinta da Alegria, the Deanery (Quinta do Deão), Quinta do Til and Sugar, Quinta da Palmeira, Quinta de Santa Luzia, Monte, Botanical Gardens, Quinta da Boa Vista, Quinta do Palheiro

Arriving

Even today, people tend to visit Madeira as much for the luxuriant vegetation, walking and magnificent scenery as to lie by a pool. (Unlike Porto Santo, Madeira is without sandy beaches.) **Mrs Charles Roundell**, travelling from England to the Azores in 1888, noted:

It is impossible to imagine a greater change in both scenery and climate than that which is experienced by travellers who, leaving England in the bitter weather of the late winter or early spring, land four days later in Madeira. Such at least was our experience.

And she observed, too, that the islanders themselves were fully conscious of the effect of floral beauty when she wrote of the Princess Maria Amélia Hospício (see 'Princess Maria Amélia' pp. 27 and 62, and 'Florence and Ella Du Cane', p. 126):

It is intended for twenty four consumptive patients of Portuguese or Brazilian birth, and stands in a lovely garden, full of every tree, shrub, and flower likely to be pleasant to the eyes of the poor invalids. The views from this garden are beautiful.

But it was not just the authorities or benefactors who added to the show; Emily Shore noted on her first visit towards the Mount:

As we went higher, we passed garden after garden, and other pieces of open ground, all filled with Madeira vegetation, which, though seen at the worst season [December], impressed us with a high idea of its luxuriance. Abundance of vine-trellises, and stone verandahs covered not only with vines, but with another luxuriant creeper, the grenadilla; geraniums growing like weeds; peach trees already in blossom; bananas; in one garden a solitary palm, and everywhere the wildest profusion of prickly pear, growing as a weed, and to a size which quite astonished us, who are used to see it cherished and yet stunted in greenhouses.

Sarah and Edward Bowdich write of the first-time visitors' feelings, particularly the well-travelled:

To those who have visited the tropics nothing can be more gratifying than to find the trees they have there dwelt on with so much pleasure, and which are decidedly the most beautiful part of Creation; to be reminded of the vast solitudes, where vegetable nature seems to reign uncontrolled and untouched; to see the bright blue sky through the delicate pinnated leaves of the mimosa, whilst the wood strawberry at its feet recalls the still dearer recollection of home; to gather the fallen guavas with one hand and the blackberry with the other; to be able to choose between the apples and cherries of Europe (which are so much regretted) and the banana — it is this feeling which makes Madeira so delightful, independent of its beautiful scenery and constancy and softness of its temperature.

Isabella de França tells us that at any grand ball of the Funchal Season flowers were to the fore:

In all cases the patio is well lighted, and hung round with the beautiful green creeper called Alegra campo, intermixed with coloured flowers, generally the orange bignonia, and the white arum. The same flowers usually decorate the rooms above, with the addition of many others, among which both red and white camellias are especially prominent, and the sweet scented heaths give a delightful fragrance to the air. The doorways are usually hung round with large wreaths, others hang on the front of the orchestra, or on the branches which support the lights. In short, wherever flowers can be placed they are in the greatest profusion, and of kinds, a single specimen of which would sell for a high price in Covent Garden.

It is tempting from those accounts to believe that flowers were appreciated by everyone in Madeira, but at the same time as Emily Shore was admiring wayside gardens in 1839, Fanny Burney Wood was receiving a contrary impression (more than ten years before Isabella de França's visit). Fanny observed on 18 October 1838:

With the exception of Dr Renton, Mr Stoddart, Mrs Gordon and Mrs Penfold, few people here appear to take any interest in the improvement and cultivation of flowers; as long as their gardens furnish them with fruit and vegetables they seem to care for nothing more. The idleness and want of energy in the upper classes strikes me every day most forcibly. The excuse made is the enervating effect of the climate, but I believe that except during the extreme heat of the summer few of *the residents born on the Island suffer from this cause* [her italics], though to strangers the effect of the change of climate is often very distressing, as I myself can fully testify.

Who she is referring to it is difficult to be sure; by upper classes it would appear that she means the Portuguese (and she rarely misses a chance to denigrate the Portuguese), but she started with a list of foreign residents and uses the term 'residents born on the island' which could mean Portuguese or long-established British mercantile families (going back at least to Catherine of Braganza's marriage to Charles II) who often led more of an upper class life than many of them would have lived in Britain.

At any rate, several foreign residents, as Fanny suggests, and as will become clear, developed exquisite gardens within their quintas. British visitors admired these, then trailed round the countryside 'botanising'; Ellen Taylor, for example was, as Edith Hutcheon notes in her book, 'that most enthusiastic of Madeira fern collectors'. But the queen of those visitors who wrote about Madeira's flora and the quinta gardens was Florence Du Cane.

Florence and Ella Du Cane

Florence (b.1869) wrote, and her sister Ella (b.1874) illustrated, *The Flowers and Gardens of Madeira*, the first edition of which was published in 1909; a more common edition, easy enough to buy on the internet, is the 1926 reprint. The first edition has 24 illustrations, the second, 16. The illustrations are rather old-fashioned (at least in reproduction), but the sisters obviously knew their onions, for Edith Hutcheon wrote in 1928:

19. Jacaranda Tree by Ella Du Cane, painted between 1899 and 1909, from Du Cane, *The Flowers and Gardens of Madeira*

The chief gardens have been very fully described by one well qualified for the task, Miss Florence Du Cane, in her book *Flowers and Gardens of Madeira*, which after being out of print for some time has been reissued, and to which the reader is referred. The book is delightfully illustrated by Miss Ella Du Cane.

If one may venture a criticism it is that the backgrounds — the glimpses of mountain and sea, and the skies — have been subordinated to an undue extent to the floral subjects. Correctly so, no doubt, from the artist's point of view, and with her objective, but failing to convey to one who does not know the Island, the jewel-bright atmosphere and vivid colouring of Madeira.

It is fortunate that Edith acknowledges being conversant with this book, for there comes a time when the modern reader wonders who is copying island historical anecdotes from whom. Even Florence Du Cane quotes from Ellen Taylor, 'a great authority on native ferns'.

Florence and Ella were both born in Hobart, Tasmania, where their father Sir Charles Du Cane was Governor until 1874; their mother was the Hon. Georgina Copley. The sisters were to travel widely and publish several books on flowers and gardens. They were in Madeira in 1899 and again in 1906. Florence shows the depths of her knowledge when she describes the gardens of the Princess Maria Amélia Hospício:

The garden is well cared for, and contains a good collection of trees and flowering shrubs. Near the entrance are some very fine *Ficus comosa* and two splendid *Jacarandas*, which, when they are laden with their blue blossoms, stand out splendidly against the dark ever-green trees; also a very large Coral-tree, whose grey leafless branches are adorned early in the year with scarlet blossoms. In the centre of the garden are two unusually fine specimens of Duranta trees, whose long hanging racemes of orange berries cause them to be much admired all through the winter and spring months, while in summer the branches are laden with their blue blossoms. Dragon-trees, frangipani-trees, judas-trees, camphor-trees, til and *Astrapea viscosa*, are all to be found here, and a large specimen of the gorgeous flame-coloured Flamboyant or Poinciana, may be easily recognized by its flat spreading branches, which shed their fern-like foliage before the blossoms appear. At all seasons of the year the garden affords a delightful pleasaunce for the inmates of the Hospital, and can never be entirely colourless, as the red dracenas and the bright crimson leaves of the acalypha, which are blotches of a lighter or darker colour, afford a welcome note of colour at all seasons of the year and a relief to the eternal green of the evergreen trees. The walls of the garden are clothed with bougainvilleas, wistarias, and other creepers, and the beds contain a variety of plants, such as clerodendrons, hibiscus, abutilons, begonias, azaleas, and roses. The grass edges to the beds give the garden a character of its own, and might well be copied in other Madeira gardens.

The history of the Hospício and details for visiting are described on pp. 28 and 62. Ella's jacaranda tree painting is my favourite of them, perhaps because I grew up with these magnificent blue-mauve confections; unfortunately, reproducing it in black and white does not do it justice, but I hope that the colour of my cover makes up for that. Jacaranda trees line Avenida Arriaga and continue in Avenida do Infante which runs past the front of the Hospício. They flower from April to June, though early birds come out in March and the blossoms can linger longer.

Florence Du Cane was just occasionally flummoxed by an island flower, which only highlights her erudition and makes it human; she wrote:

There are several roses which are to be found in most of the gardens to which I could never put a name: one in particular I can recall, with a beautiful clear, bright pink blossom, touched with a deeper red on the back of the petals, which I frequently admired and endeavoured to get correctly named; but no one knew its name, and at last a friend said: 'Why worry about its name? We just call it "The most beautiful rose that grows"' — and it seemed indeed a good name for it.

Quinta da Achada

In the nineteenth century, there was an arc of quintas just to the north of Funchal. I am not suggesting that you visit in an arc the ones whose history and gardens are now described; they may fit naturally into other interests and activities. All have an interesting past but not all, in their current manifestation, are open to the public.

To the west was the Quinta da Achada. *Achada* simply means a level tract of land on the top or side of high ground and this quinta was built on a promontory high above the Ribeira de Santa Luzia. As Florence Du Cane was to write in 1909, 'The Achada has ... long been famous for its garden and grounds. It formerly belonged to an English family, who probably planted most of the rare trees, palms, and Dracaenas, and the large magnolia trees for which it has become famous.' She is referring to the Penfold family.

Unless I pause here and explain the Penfolds, muddle could ensue. The Madeira wine merchant William Penfold (b.1776) married **Sarah Gilbert** (b.1776). They had seven children, several of whom feature in this chapter. Their eldest daughter, Emma, married George Stoddart and is Mrs Stoddart in quotations that follow. Their eldest son, William Burton, married **Clara Houghton**, daughter of a wine merchant, and she thus becomes a second Mrs Penfold. Their daughter **Augusta June** (d.1869) married Captain John Horatio **Robley** (1838) and published as Mrs Robley. Their daughter Jane Wallas married William Mathews in 1846 but, therefore, published in 1845 as **Jane Wallas Penfold**.

The rather charming story is told of how Jane Wallas Penfold was sliding down the banisters when she sent a visitor flying – **Caroline of Brunswick** (1768–1821) estranged wife of the future George IV of England. Young Jane obviously made her mark, being presented in due course with a diamond brooch.

William Penfold senior died early in our story (1835), but his wife Sarah lived long thereafter (d.1886) at Quinta da Achada – so sometimes Mrs Penfold must be Sarah Gilbert, and sometimes Clara Houghton.

Fanny Burney Wood visited the Quinta da Achada in 1838 and wrote on 24 December:

To-day in Mrs Penfold's garden I saw a really magnificent South-American Creeper (Tecoma venusta), in full blossom over some trellis work. It makes a superb appearance, and at a distance is one mass of deep rich colour, surpassing in brilliancy any flower I have ever seen. There are also handsome variegated Bamboo (with striped leaves), and a Fiddle Plant, and, in the vineyard, the Sugar-cane.

I know this is Sarah, Mrs Penfold senior, recently widowed, because Fanny goes on to mention her daughter Mrs Stoddart. Two of Sarah's other daughters were known for their floral paintings. In 1845, Jane Wallas Penfold published *Madeira: Flowers, Fruits and Ferns*. It is not easy to track down and I wish I could say it is worth it when you succeed but to me the paintings, of rather uninteresting flowers and fruit, seem muddy and undistinguished, though they must have been admired and my views are not universally shared.

One of the watercolours by Miss Penfold in the Emily Smith folio at Quinta das Cruzes (see p. 102) – two rather unappetising bananas – is almost identical to one of these illustrations. Perhaps they should all be seen as a botanical record, rather than artistic endeavour.

In the front of Jane's book is a poem called 'Song of Madeira' by Mrs Calverley Bewicke. **Mary Bewicke**, who had lived in Madeira for four years because of her husband's health, started the poem 'We dwellers in a fairy land ...' It has to be said that she is more distinguished by being the mother of a girl who grew up in Madeira to be the turn-of-the century feminist novelist A.N. Bewicke and, later, Mrs Archibald Little, an Old China Hand and writer about China, than by her own poetry. Eagerly I sought a Madeira setting to a novel by **Alicia Bewicke** (1845–1925), but in vain! Her most autobiographical, *Miss Standish* (1898), looks as if the heroine is nostalgic for balmy days in Madeira, but it turns out to be the Italian Riviera.

Another poem in Jane Penfold's book, specially written for it, is by the Poet Laureate, William Wordsworth, so she had, at least, connections. Among the subscribers behind the publication is Jane's sister Augusta. That same year, as **Mrs Robley**, she published *A Selection of Madeira Flowers* which unhappily creates much the same impression as Jane's work. Standards for such paintings have been set rather high, I'm afraid, by Marianne North who was so briefly in Madeira. She did not, unfortunately, leave any paintings of the island among her magnificent collection at Kew Gardens.

The Penfolds had been firm supporters of the Reverend Richard Lowe in the early days of his ministry and he, in turn, wrote of

Women's Places

Sarah Penfold that in her 'We have the most assiduous of practical gardeners.' And, even in 1845, when Jane's book was published, she could write in the preface, 'To the Rev. R.T. Lowe, whose name is so well known to scientific men in connection with the natural history of Madeira, and to the Hon. C.E.C. Norton, I am under obligations for much valuable assistance.' (See p. 102.)

I suspect that the Penfold women may have stayed above the Lowe fray, but not so their brother William Burton Penfold who was elected treasurer of the Church at the meeting in 1847 that stopped Lowe's salary and was thus a member of the formal anti-Lowe triumvirate. A clue to his change of loyalty may lie not so much in the changing of generations – his father died in 1835 – as in the link by marriage in 1835 between the Penfolds and Charles Blandy, one of Lowe's leading adversaries. Blandy married Sarah Penfold's niece **Mary Anne Symonds** (1808–1891) (see p. 22).

When Florence Du Cane praised the Quinta da Achada gardens and the English family that had nurtured them, she continued, 'The property then changed hands, and for some years belonged to a Portuguese family, but it is now again in English hands.' When and how the Penfolds gave it up is unclear but in 1881 it was bought by Adolphus Lindon who came to Madeira for six months with tuberculosis and lived for another 20 years becoming, in the meantime, Archdeacon of the Islands. During his initial convalescence, he met and married a visitor from Alsace, Laurie Mieg, and they continued to develop the gardens. The gardening mantle was taken on by their daughter and granddaughter.

Elia Lindon (1884–1958) was born at Quinta da Achada. She served as a nurse in Serbia during the First World War and met there a French doctor, Raymond Monier-Vinard, whom she married. After their marriage, they lived mainly in Paris but she returned often to Quinta da Achada. The Monier-Vinards were trapped in Paris in the Second World War during which Elia was active in the Resistance. She was widowed before the end, in 1943, and after Liberation, she and her daughter **Sylvie** (1923–1979) made their way home through Lisbon to Madeira. They set to again on the garden at the quinta.

In 1946, Sylvie married John Reeder Blandy, the younger son of that generation, as his second wife. She had taken an agricultural course in France and, once the water was restored at the quinta, she developed the vegetable gardens there into a business, supplying produce to, for example, Reid's Hotel – owned since 1937 by the Blandy family – though she and John did not live there permanently until some years after her mother's death in 1958.

In 1979 Sylvie's second son, Edward, inherited the quinta but he died young and his widow, **Georgina** (née **Bickford**), eventually went into partnership to convert it into the Jardins do Lago Hotel, named for the large lake which is such a feature. The gardens which the Penfold and Monier-Vinard women so loved still provide pleasure.

Quinta da Alegria

Only one of Fanny Burney Wood's Madeira sketches is included in the book of her journals: 'The Ravine of the Fairies'. She does not locate the sketch in the caption, nor have I come across another mention of its subject. A clue to the whereabouts of the ravine is contained in her entry of 9 May 1839 when she visited Mrs Penfold's rented cottage at Alegria, 'the opposite ravine to the Mount', on the 'Marquis de Torrebella's estate'. Fanny observed, 'What a pretty spot it is! The little house stands in the midst of a chestnut Wood under which grow the beautiful Bella Donna Lily and the pink Oxalis in great profusion.' (Is that Mrs Penfold Clara Houghton?)

Later that day, 'We sallied forth upon another ramble to the little waterfall, a trifling affair, which the people say is haunted by "Feiticeiras," or Fairies. They affirm that these invisible beings frequently lead unwary mortals astray into brakes and briars, and tear their clothes.'

With the only clues the names 'Alegria' and 'Torrebella', we set off one hot morning to São Roque, past what was Quinta da Achada and on the way to Alegria. There, just above São Roque, beyond obvious

20. 'The Ravine of the Fairies', Quinta Alegria, by Fanny Burney Wood 1838/39, from Rolt, *A Great-Niece's Journals*

signs of continuing development, we found a house still called Quinta da Alegria, though not quite as I imagined it. We walked along in front of the house to a neglected bit of land round a dilapidated stone hut; beyond that we looked down into the Ribeira de Santa Luzia. There, with no one else about, we could almost imagine fairies. And, across Funchal, down below, the view to the sea was stunning.

To the north of that land which lay to the side and behind the house, was a fence against which stood two copper beech trees. Beyond the fence was thick woodland and behind that a water pumping station. With the help of our taxi driver and a neighbour working on his new house, our quest was explained to a local man, Antonio Freitas. He insisted that we drive up to the water pumping station and then climb up a path beyond, and through what had obviously once been a well-tended vegetable garden and orchard. Then, through the undergrowth, he pointed out some ruins which he believed were what we were looking for.

A few weeks later, I talked in England to a member of the family that owned much of this area for many generations, including the time of the Penfolds' stay. She knows it is much changed and at first hardly recognised my description. But she filled in some of the gaps around the quinta as it was and is now and what I already knew of her ancestors.

The Torre Bella family, on whose estate this house stood and who, indeed, built it, is itself of interest to us: because of a consistent lack of male heirs, the title **de Torre Bella** and the family estates have descended through the female line since 1875 when they were inherited by the second Visconde's daughter, **Dona Filomena Gabriela Correia Brandão Henriques de Noronha** (1839–1925). She was another Portuguese woman who, by force of circumstance, managed large domains. She married Russell Manners Gordon in 1857 and they too only had daughters. The family and, thus, the title (created 1812) have been distilled by marriage to become informally Scottish-Irish rather than Portuguese. In 1974, Dermot **Bolger**, the last male heir, and his wife died within months of each other. That same year, the Portuguese Revolution took place and the new government commenced the redistribution of land, including that in Madeira. Two Torre Bella daughters, **Ann** (later Fairlie) and **Susan** (later Seldon), were left with two family quintas.

Ann continued to live at the family's summer retreat, Quinta da Alegria, where she had, in 1970, planted two copper beech trees brought over from her garden at Myers Castle in Scotland. She was a knowledgeable and keen gardener. But in 1986 she died unexpectedly and the quinta was sold. The current Quinta da Alegria, perhaps somewhat changed, seems to be where Fanny visited the Penfolds. The stone hut was the cowshed which was converted for the two Torre Bella girls as their own place when the family returned to Madeira after the Second World War. As for the ruins beyond the wood, that is a mystery! The Viscondessa Torre Bella, the last of her line, lives in England without using the title.

That aspect of the family is looking forward in time from Filomena; looking back from her is interesting too. When her grandfather inherited, the family owned vast lands in Madeira. Earlier than that, the vineyards at São Roque and, indeed, the Torre Bella family itself, seem to have been connected to Dona Guiomar and her commercial empire. Her second brother's second wife, **Antonia Joana Correia Henriques** (m.1765), was a Torre Bella, as was **Ana Inâcia Betencourt Henriques** who also married into Dona Guiomar's family. It is fair to suggest, therefore, that all this area may once have formed part of Dona Guiomar's properties (see p. 13). It was not just fairies we could think of there. But the encroaching of development suggests that it may well not be worth a visit in future.

The Deanery (Quinta do Deão)

Across the ravine from Quinta da Achada, was the Deanery (also known as Quinta do Deão). When **Emma Penfold** (c.1803–1892) married George **Stoddart**, she became responsible for the Deanery gardens, though the house itself was usually let – the family lived elsewhere, including at Monte (see pp. 129 and 143–8). Fanny Burney Wood notes on 1 October 1838 that,

Mrs Stoddart has kindly given me permission to walk in the garden of the 'Deanery' ... whenever I please while it remains untenanted. The air there is scented with the beautiful perfume of the abundant fruit on the Orange trees, which are very large and healthy.

Among the rare trees at the Deanery is the Silk Cotton, which flowers every year; the Plumiera Rubra (the beautiful buff and pink blossoms have a delicious scent resembling the smell of Apricots); the Pitanga from Brazil, the fruit of which is sweet with a slightly smoky taste; and elegant species of Pine from the Himalaya Mountains, the seed of which was given to Mr Stoddart by Lady Amherst.

On 18 October 1838, after again going to the Deanery Gardens, Fanny confides to her diary, 'To-day I have commenced a Book of Sketches of all the Madeira flowers, plants and fruits, which will, in future years, be a memorial of my visit to this beautiful Island.'

Her granddaughter, Margaret S. Rolt, editing her diaries for their 1926 publication, adds in a footnote, 'This Album, bound in dark morocco leather, contains numerous beautifully painted sketches of the plants and flowers found in Madeira; the drawings are as fresh as if just executed.' But she does not say where that album is – which becomes increasingly frustrating, particularly when Fanny tells us that she sketched in such places as the Santa Clara Convent. However, the Deanery was obviously a fine place in which, and from which, to sketch, for here is Lady Susan Harcourt's view. All we have from Fanny Burney Wood of Madeira is 'The Ravine of the Fairies' (see 'Quinta da Alegria', p. 133).

By 1880, when Ellen Taylor visited Madeira, Emma was living as a widow at the Deanery. Florence Du Cane wrote of it 20 years later:

The Deanery, standing in a very sheltered situation at the foot of the Santa Luzia ravine, has proved an admirable trial-ground for trees, shrubs, and plants which have been collected by its present owner. From all parts of the world rare and interesting plants have been brought, and some have been raised from seed on the spot.

Florence goes on to quote an anonymous 1825 writer which sounds to me like a woman: 'To-day we have removed to Deanery, our Country-house ... our great luxury ... is the garden. It is one of the largest and most beautiful in the island.' Frustratingly, Florence does not say where she found this account but it does suggest that it was neither Emma Penfold Stoddart, nor her successor, who was originally responsible for the Deanery's beauty.

After Emma's death, the Deanery became the property of Charles O.L. Power and his wife, **Gertrude Frances Power**. Charles Power and his son, Charles, are well known – father apparently for the garden at the Deanery, and his son for a guide book of Madeira. Perhaps less well-known is the younger man's sister **Sheila Mary Power** (1903–1971), described in the Madeira biographical dictionary as 'musician, composer, poet and writer.'

Sheila Power gave concerts – composing and playing – at the Quinta do Deão for 30 years for friends and music lovers, and even

21. View from the Deanery by Lady Susan Harcourt, 1851, from Harcourt, *Sketches in Madeira*

attracted foreign artists. Her talents were further developed when she became close friends with Marion Shanks who lived at Quinta do Pico da Pedra at Monte and wrote plays. The two of them began to collaborate on musical dramas.

Marion Shanks (née Champness, 1904–1960), whose father had made a fortune from a welding patent, was married with five children. She had first come to Madeira in 1933, without her husband, for her son's convalescence from pneumonia. She became part of Funchal's jetset and, in due course, a permanent resident. At her quinta she, too, made use of her artistic talents; in the summer of 1940, for example, 'The Pico Players' presented a song and ballet performance of 'Undine', adapted and produced by Marion, the players including some of her children. By 1942, Sheila Power had moved from the Deanery to live with Marion at Monte. There they composed, wrote and produced together.

Probably following a production of their drama 'São Bernadino's Chapel', attended by the Bishop and priests, their partnership developed into a religious foundation – the Order of Good Will in Christ. One day each week they opened the garage at Quinta Pico to feed hundreds of Monte's poor and they could sometimes be seen in Funchal in patched and darned nuns' habits. Eventually, they transferred their lives, and their Order, to Portugal.

Meanwhile, the Deanery had been sold. One of my informants remembers it when she was a girl in the 1950s – a lovely house with huge trees, as if set in a park. One day her father noticed that it was being pulled down and managed to rescue some fine fireplaces. Today, when you drive up Rua do Deão, you are confronted by a road lined, on the right, with a phalanx of apartment blocks.

Quinto do Til and Sugar

Ellen Taylor notes in 1880 that 'Gardening is a great resource in Madeira, and many ladies devote much thought and attention to it.' She adds that to the younger Miss Hinton at Quinta do Til 'must be awarded the palm for great excellence and success in the perfect flowers she cultivated with such pleasure and perseverance'.

Miss Hinton was a member of another Madeira commercial dynasty, tangentially connected with the Penfolds. William Penfold was successor in a wine firm to Robert Wallas, married to **Jane Burnett** (1782–1848); their daughter, **Mary Wallas** (1819–1888) married William Hinton. Miss Hinton was their daughter. Hinton traded first in wine and flour, as well as encouraging the development of the wicker craft in Camacha where they also had a quinta. Later he concentrated on sugar, a business which his son, Harry, expanded.

Sugar was as profitable a commodity in its day as wine; indeed, sugar growing predated vineyards and wine making. The earliest plantations – for which slaves were brought in (see also pp. 81–4) – were cane growing and sugar producing. Many of the European foreigners, such as the Acciaiuolis, Bettencourts, Drummonds, Lomelinos and Franças, came to Madeira in the fifteenth and mid-sixteenth centuries to make their fortunes in this commodity. They were well-versed in European high finance and had contacts in the main trading centres. Their money-making flair attracted the island's Portuguese aristocracy, and marriage with a dowry was a way of acquiring, and then expanding, land and becoming part of island society.

The industrial revolution saw the introduction of steam-driven sugar mills and the end of slavery, but there was also a crisis in the sugar market. During the eighteenth and early nineteenth centuries, the only functioning sugar mill was in the Ribeira dos Socorridos – not surprisingly, it belonged to Dona Guiomar (see p. 12) who rented it out to a relative for a considerable sum.

Sugar was to be used for spirit (rum) and later for beer, but one of its primary uses, as early as the fifteenth century, was for preserves and confectionery, including dried fruits, crystallised citrus rind and jam. Madeira's sugar products were highly esteemed throughout Europe. Thanks to women in both town and country, production of these comestibles ensured the survival of many a family.

The nuns of the Santa Clara, Encarnação and Mercês Convents were to become famous, and richer, for their making and selling of confectionery. They also consumed a lot of sugar themselves, in the form of fritters, potato sweets, cheese cakes, sweet rice and cakes. The only remnant of this industry is the Madeira honey cake – Bolo de Mel – made from sugar cane molasses. Don't expect a jar of honey when you buy *mel* (honey), but the cakes are pretty good! William and Harry Hinton were, in due time, a major part of this industry and had some tussles with their Madeiran competitors as a result.

In 1908 Harry Hinton bought Quinta da Palmeira above Quinta do Til and we shall visit that next. It may well be that his sister, Miss Hinton, whose first name is so far lost, was still in charge when Florence Du Cane explained why the Til garden was so fine:

The garden is very sheltered, and never seems to suffer from the strong, rough winds which those in a more exposed and open situation feel so keenly. Here comes no rude blast from the east to strip the leaves off the great begonia plants, and their brittle foliage and heavy flower-heads remain unbruised and untorn, while many a neighbouring garden has suffered severely at the hands of a winter storm ...

It is evident that this garden is tended with loving hands, and all the necessary alterations and pruning are done under the close supervision of its owners ... The lower terrace is almost entirely a rose-garden, the Til garden having always been famous for its roses.

Harry Hinton had a goddaughter, **Margaret Cossart** (1910–1979), and when she married Cecil Miles he enabled the young couple to buy Quinta do Til cheaply. It has now left the Miles family and has a Portuguese owner. Although it is private property, you can get a feeling of it by driving slowly down Rua do Til (before you turn into Rua do Deão) and looking left. You will see some fine wrought iron gates alongside which the bougainvillea and other abundant flora spill over the low wall.

Quinta da Palmeira

Florence Du Cane wrote of Quinta da Palmeira at the time of Harry Hinton's purchase of it:

Just above [Quinta do Til], on the Levada de Santa Luzia, is the gate of the Quinta Palmeira, which takes its name from the large palm-tree which rears its head proudly and stands alone in the grounds. The path leading to the house winds up the side of the hill, through grounds which for many years had been out of cultivation, until the property changed hands a short time ago; but as the ground had always been left in more or less its wild and natural state, it suffered less than if it had been a cultivated garden.

It is a beautiful piece of rocky ground, and on one side a group of *Pinus pinea*, stone, or parasol pines, stand towering over a grand cliff which rises abruptly from the river-bed.

Hinton's second wife, in 1926, was **Isabel Beatriz da Câmara Vasconcelos Couto Cardoso Bettencourt** (1872–1945) who had left her husband João Welsh for him. It was Isabel who, in the early 1930s, laid out the formal gardens at Palmeira incorporating the fine established trees. She is also remembered on her tombstone in the

British Cemetery for her good works – for helping the sick and poor (see p. 78).

Since Harry Hinton had no children by either of his wives, Isabel's son by her first marriage, George Welsh, inherited both his commercial interests and Quinta da Palmeira. His wife, a New Zealander, **Theo Beswick** (1901–1996), was another keen and enterprising gardener who corresponded internationally to enhance what Isabel had initiated. Theo's mother, **Florence E. Beswick** (d.1967), was an accomplished artist, painting Madeira flowers and scenes in oil.

Isabel ('**Binkie**') **Welsh**, Theo and George's daughter, lay down in front of bulldozers when the government recently appropriated the old Hinton sugar mill, with its tall landmark chimney, just below Quinta do Til, and started demolishing it.

In 2003, the gardens of Quinta da Palmeira were opened to the public (Monday to Friday, 9.00a.m.–12.00p.m. and 2.00p.m.– 5.00p.m.). The Welsh family no longer live in the house which there are plans to restore and open.

Quinta de Santa Luzia

Next in the west to east arc of quintas is the Quinta de Santa Luzia – the Blandy family home for generations. It was from Santa Luzia in 1866 that Fanny Blandy had signalled to the scientist who was to become her husband and Lord Kelvin (see p. 47). The houses on this extensive property then belonged to her parents, Charles Ridpath Blandy and Mary Anne Symonds, and a photograph exists of the large family reading and sewing in a comfortable room on the floor of which lies a tiger skin over rugs from the Orient.

Florence Du Cane wrote of Santa Luzia at the turn of the century:

The palm must be given to the garden of Santa Luzia, as not only does it cover a much larger expanse of ground than any other, but when owners take so much individual interest in almost every plant in the garden, as here everything seems to flourish and grow at its best, for flowers grow better for those who love them.

Like all good gardeners, they have not been deterred by the failure of a plant one season or the failure to import a new treasure at the first attempt, but have given hosts of plants a fair trial, often rewarded with success in the end, though naturally failing in some cases. Plants have been sent to them from all parts of the world, and the island owes many of its flowering treasures to this garden, which was originally their nursery and trial ground.

You begin to see that, in different ways, Florence gave the palm to each quinta in turn, thus pleasing all owners, and offending none of her hosts. Discreetly or not wishing her account to date, she names none of them. The quinta then belonged to John Burden Blandy who married for the second time in 1882. Following his death in 1912, his widow, **Alice Berrington**, lived in Madeira until 1919 when she returned to England, dying in 1929. It is assumed that she tended the garden at least until 1901, when her stepson, John Ernest, married the American **Elinor Olds Reeder** (1875–1961). Elinor was certainly a keen gardener and Santa Luzia owes much to her.

John Burden Blandy had, by the time of the Du Cane visit, bought Quinta do Palheiro (see p. 156) which, on his death in 1912, his elder son inherited. Although Santa Luzia then went to the younger son of the next generation, John Reeder Blandy, his widowed mother, Elinor, lived on in the house for another 30 years. At some stage her daughter-in-law, Sylvie Monier-Vinard, further developed the vegetable gardens on the quinta's farm, as she did her mother's at Quinta da Achada (see p. 132). Santa Luzia has now passed to the next generation. Today, as you drive down Rua de Santa Luzia from Monte, you pass, on your right, a high, buff-coloured wall – again, you can catch a glimpse.

Monte

Rua de Santa Luzia leads up to Monte (sometimes called the Mount) and you can now go there easily by road. When Mary Phelps lived there in the mid-nineteenth century, you usually went from your town house to your Monte quinta on horseback. If you were a visitor, there were other means of transport. Fanny Burney Wood writes on 2 October 1838 how,

This morning we set off in three Palanquins to spend the day at Bello Monte, Mr Stoddart's Quinta, near the Mount Church. The cool shady grounds reminded me of the woods of dear old England, but I soon remembered that I was in a foreign land when I looked at the beautiful Bella Donna lilies and large white Arum (Calla aethiopica) growing wild at my feet. Miss Penfold tells me that these flowers are as abundant in woods and waste lands here as the common Arum, or Adder's Tongue, in England. I sketched a magnificent Dragon Tree, a splendid Portugal Laurel — (a forest-tree in size) — and a Gum tree, new to me.

Isabella de França describes her visit to the Stoddarts in 1853 by way of a *carro de bois*, or ox sledge, three miles up to Monte. Sitting back to front, they passed 'geraniums, fuchsias, heliotrope, Coronella and wild rose', wild by the road or hanging over rough stone walls. George Stoddart, the British Consul, was an old friend of her husband; his wife was Emma Penfold (see pp. 129 and 135).

22. Isabella de França ascending Monte in an ox sledge, 1853, courtesy of Frederico de Freitas Museum

Today, at least once, you must go up to Monte by the cable car (opened in 2000) which departs from the promenade in the Old Town. People who live on its route are incensed by the intrusion into their privacy and I'm not surprised because how can you avoid sticky beaking into every alley and window as you rise gently upwards? It is a stupendous ride, climbing and descending – with the whole of Funchal, its amphitheatre of mountains and the sea, spread out for your delectation.

One of my searches on the ten minute ride was for where exactly Isabella de França was made to clamber up a mountainside when visiting another of her husband's properties. Not long after they had reached Monte in a *carro de bois* on another day, the poor oxen were in such difficulty that Isabella insisted on getting down. It would be hard to say that she continued the journey on foot, for she wrote:

The Feitor (bailiff) had gone up with us, and led the way, with his iron pointed mountain staff, expecting me to follow; José walked behind, to catch me if I fell, but up at that dizzy height, in the heat of a burning Sun, and with a perpendicular precipice on each side of me, I lost all power of keeping upright, and finding that I could neither go forward nor retreat, I went down on my hands and knees and crawled over the rocks, sometimes clinging to a friendly piece of broom, sometimes guided by the Feitor's hand, when I was lucky enough to reach it, and often looking back, when I dared, to see where José was, and how he was getting on. This perilous path was at last passed, and we arrived at the pine trees, which are planted on a precipice hanging over the Ribeira de João Gomes; it was difficult to stand when we got there, for the trees are planted on so steep an acclivity, that it was only by clinging from one tree to another, that I could make my way in amongst them. My Husband gathered a cone for me, to bring home as a trophy, and I also picked up one of the fallen sprays of the pine trees, called in Portuguese a 'França'; the ground was so covered with these fallen sprays that it was almost too slippery to stand upon, and added to the steepness of the ground, made it almost impossible to avoid falling.

You will have fun, I hope, as you rise above the Ribeira de João Gomes (which bends eastwards), speculating where exactly Isabella

23.   Isabella de França above Ribeira de João Gomes, 1853, courtesy of Frederico de Freitas Museum

was taken. Even today it would, I suspect, be gruelling, though all this is walking area, well-described in relevant guides.

Visitors to Madeira go to Monte for three things – apart from walking: the gardens, the church and the toboggan ride down. Dominating the landscape, even from below, is Nossa Senhora do Monte Church on the site of the chapel built by Eve and Adam in 1470 (see pp. 3–4). Soon after, a shepherd girl from nearby Terreiro da Luta claimed to have seen a vision of the Virgin Mary. A small sculpture of the virgin was found there and was later transferred to the Monte Church. In 1927, a huge statue – Our Lady of Peace – was erected in Terreiro da Luta (three kilometres' steep climb beyond Monte, or a quick drive), following prayers to the Virgin during the First World War.

Prayers had been said to the Virgin of the Mount in 1803, during the devastating flood which killed over 300 people (see p. 44); after that she became the island's much-revered patron saint. Emily Smith incorporates all these aspects in her diary account of an outing on 8 December 1841 from the Phelps' Quinta Prazer at the Mount.

Mr Phelps' Quinta is at an elevation of 1700 feet and just 300 feet lower than the Mount Church; we walked about his grounds wh[ich] are lovely; terrace above terrace with all sorts of curious trees ... Dragon trees, giant Cactus, Vinhatigo or Mahogany tree, innumerable orange and lemon trees. [After we dined at 2] we walked to the side of a fine Ravine called the little Curral & saw where the torrent had come down wh inundated Funchal in 1803, & carried away bridges, houses etc. We then went to the Mount Church whence the view is magnificent. It is a Singular edifice & Nossa Senhora del Monte is daily installed at the great high Altar. We then walked down another Ravine by a waterfall, the Spring of water where the legend is founded about finding a statue of the Virgin. The scenery was lovely & the path wound charmingly along the ravine till we came back to Mr Phelps'.

I am trying to set the scene, rather spectacularly, for how you place in your mind's eye, and in reality, the quintas of the Phelps and Stoddarts and where the ex-Empress Zita of Austria nursed her husband dying of pneumonia in 1922 as you set about visiting Monte.

In January 1839, Emily Shore rode up to Monte, in spite of her fragility, and wrote:

As I proceeded upwards, the hedge-banks became crowned with walnut-trees, and clothed with myrtles, aloes, broom, ivy, brambles, geraniums, laurel, stonecrops, and many other plants, both native and Madeirense. A turn to the left, not far below the church, brought me suddenly to the brink of a precipice overlooking a great ravine, that spreads out gradually as it reached Funchal. On the right were the garden walls of the thickly wooded quintas of Mr Stoddart and Mr Phelps; on the left was the abrupt undefended precipice, nearly perpendicular, and perhaps four hundred feet in height.

Fifty or so years later, Florence Du Cane passed that way and wrote:

Not many years ago the ground which is now the beautiful garden of the Palace Hotel was nothing but rocky, waste ground, bare of vegetation, except for the clumps of prickly-pear, agaves, and cacti which take possession of all the rocky ground along the shore. For situation the garden is unrivalled, and though the garden lacks the care and attention which naturally are bestowed on a private garden, the luxuriant growth, especially of the creepers, has converted the formerly waste ground into a beautiful jungle of flowers. The garden is devoid of any fine trees, except for the ficus trees, a few oaks, and a stray cypress or two which surround the Dépendence, which was formerly a private house; it stands at the very edge of the precipitous cliff where the unceasing roar of the surf rings in one's ears as it dashes almost against its very walls. In front of the main building are some large cabbage palms, affording welcome shade and shelter, which have made astonishingly rapid growth, as only ten years ago they were merely items in flower-beds, and I little thought that on my second visit to the island, some seven years later, they would become an important feature in the garden.

We need to go back now to the eighteenth century. Then, Charles Murray, British Consul between 1772 and 1779, and his wife **Isabel Seat**, acquired all this area and lived in a property called Quinta do Monte. They sold the whole estate in 1798 and its new Portuguese owners divided it. In 1805, Phelps, Page & Company purchased one part, called Quinta Prazer ('Pleasure'). This was the Phelps' quinta, the grounds much beautified by Mrs Phelps, until 1847 when they sold it.

I have been unable to establish the location of their country estate between then and when they left Madeira in the early 1860s. It matters because of Bella's setting up of the embroidery industry in the early 1850s (see pp. 29–30). I suspect it may have been another quinta further to the west, near Santana (not to be confused with the better-known Santana to the north-east of the island), since that is where Bella is said to have taught children in an orphanage attached to a convent.

Neither have I been able to find Quinta Prazer itself. That is not entirely surprising. The family member who started to transcribe Mary Phelps' diaries (**N.V. Oakley**, descendent by marriage of Mary's sister Clara) went, as she says in her draft foreword to the transcription, looking for the quinta on a visit to Madeira probably some time before the Second World War. She wrote, 'I never found the Mount [Quinta Prazer] though we climbed many paths into the hilly interior'.

As for the Stoddart's Quinta Bello Monte, that is the nearest down from the church. At one stage it became the Grand Hotel Belmonte; now it is part of a school. If, just below the church, you go to where the toboggan ride starts, you will see an arch with that inscription. If you are inclined, or intrusive enough, you can find your way through the grounds of the modern part of the school to what was the Stoddart's quinta itself. A low box-hedge maze is still kept trim and palm trees stand against the imposing white house with its columns and double encircling balcony; from the right angle, the church can be seen towering above. What Florence Du Cane meant by a 'Dépendence' – outbuilding – I cannot explain, unless it is the Bello Monte. The house fronts onto the Caminho do Monte where there is a locked gate near the north-west entrance/exit of the Tropical Gardens. Be careful not to dawdle in the road, as you could be brought low by a toboggan which gathers speed there.

Quinta do Monte, or Mount House, itself is over the other side (eastwards), on a ridge just above the cable car station. It was built in the 1820s by the merchant David Webster Gordon and his gardener wife and was known as Quinta do Monte or Quinta Gordon, then Quinta Cossart when it became one of the Cossart family's country homes. In 1921, it was still a private quinta and was lent to the exiled Emperor Karl and Empress Zita of Austria; there they stayed during his final illness. As a result it became known as Quinta dos Jardins do Imperador. He is buried in Monte Church and she returned over the years to visit his grave (see p. 68).

More recently, the quinta was acquired by the government to form part of Madeira University. Instead, I'm told, plans are afoot to convert it into high-class tourist accommodation.

As far as the 'palace' in the tropical gardens is concerned, that has little connection with any of our women. The whole area was acquired in 1897, and the palace then built. It was later converted into the Monte Palace Hotel – that mentioned by Florence Du Cane – and it is now a private 'house'. The gardens surrounding it are, however, a public park – the Tropical Gardens of Monte Palace (entered just to the left of the cable car terminus and open daily from 9.00 a.m. to 6.00 p.m.). They are well worth a visit. Don't miss some pleasing sculptures – the Skipping Girl on the terrace in front of the house and, to the west, my favourite, 'Coming with the Wind' – a mother and daughter running joyfully across the roof of the world.

The Phelps' Quinta Prazer must, I think, have been in the lower part of what are now the Tropical Gardens. The family could easily visit the Gordons and take visitors to the 'Little Curral'. This is also known as the Curral dos Romeiros and is to the east of Monte. It is at the head of the Ribeira de João Gomes and it is here that Isabella de França clambered. Today, walking guides (see bibliography) show you the route all round this area, often via *levadas*, the artificial mountain water courses so much a feature of upland Madeira and upon which its lower vegetation depends.

Botanical Gardens (Quinta do Bom Sucesso)

On the eastern hillside of the Funchal amphitheatre, about two miles from the city centre, reached by the same road as Monte, are the government-owned Botanical Gardens (sometimes known as Quinta do Bom Sucesso). They were established in 1960 and house more than 2,000 plants, of which 100 are indigenous. Within these grounds is the house that in 1982 became the Natural History Museum containing specimens of the myriad fish drawn by Sarah Bowdich, Caroline Norton and Mary Young.

Madeira's fish are still regarded as special. In the twentieth century, **Hermione Blandy de Freitas Martins** (1907–1973) and her husband had a floating tank anchored off Santa Cruz, where they had their weekend house Quinta Reveredo (see p. 37), and invited local fisherfolk to dump into it anything they thought interesting. Every fortnight or so, the tank was towed to Funchal to meet the 'homeward-bound' Union Castle liner. The fish ended up in the aquarium of Regent's Park Zoo, London. (Hermione also climbed Alpine peaks – the first woman up one of them – drove a powerful two-seater Ford up and down Madeira's heights and had a passion for dogs, latterly Great Danes – sometimes as many as five at a time.)

For 75 years or so, Quinta do Bom Sucesso was better known as Quinta Reid and housed a large extended family. The paterfamilias died in 1888 but in 1892 young William Reid brought his new bride **Caroline de Seilan**, thereafter known as Carrie, to join the household; soon she had created a menagerie in the grounds. Her niece Tommy wrote:

Part of the Quinta garden became full of aviaries and cages housing about a dozen monkeys of various kinds, numerous marmoset parrots and parakeets, several macaws and more than three hundred and fifty small birds. My aunt, I believe earned quite a place for herself among the fancy by becoming the first person to breed a Grey African parrot in captivity.

But the star turn was Ambrose, either a warthog or a Brazilian capybara, 'a creature rather like an enormous and grotesque guinea-pig who spent his time grubbing around in the wake of the gardeners'. But he had an even more endearing characteristic, as Tommy describes:

24. Clara Reid's family (Tommy left) at Quinta do Bom Sucesso, c. 1896, courtesy of Anne Evans Bohme

Ambrose was a great music lover. He was, moreover, incurably sentimental. Should he hear the piano being played in the drawing-room, he would trot from the farthest limits of the fazenda, to listen. On one occasion a well-known Russian pianist who was staying at Reid's Hotel, came to tea with my mother and to play on the Quinta's

Bechstein grand-piano, a particularly fine instrument. After playing for some time, the Russian lady turned towards the french-windows which led onto the verandah, to find herself gazing into the eyes of a sawny [soppy] looking water-hog, which lay with his head against the glass, entranced and overcome with inexpressible emotion. Delighted, the Russian lady played again, especially for Ambrose.

Clara's daughters, Tommy, Patricia and Margaret, learnt to play on that piano, taught by their governess **Fraulein Fuchs** who had been a pupil of Liszt. Fraulein Fuchs had come to Madeira with the family of **Princess** (**Pelagia**?) **Sapieha** (1844–1929); when they left, as Tommy explains,

She stayed on to start her school, all the lessons being given in German or French as her English was poor.

After teaching for some time in a room in the grounds of the Santa Clara Hotel, my father installed her as our governess in a pretty little cottage in the fazenda of the Quinta Reid, where she lived with her fourteen cats and her grand-piano until the War of 1914, when she left for the Azores. There she died during an outbreak of plague.

Fraulein Fuchs taught Tommy fluent German, French and music; painting she learnt from her mother's friend, the artist Ella Du Cane (see p. 125).

Another Quinta Reid character was the parlour maid **Francisca**, 'a strikingly handsome woman'. One evening at a dinner party, a rat ran among the guests. When the panic had subsided, Francisca was left silent and very pale standing on a table circled by dogs. 'On my mother asking her whether she was alright,' Tommy remembered, 'Francisca said "Ask the gentlemen to leave the room Senhora, and I will tell you". My mother did so, on which Francisca said "the rat is up my drawers". What self control and what a perfect servant!'

Today when you visit the Botanical Gardens, the gardens themselves are, of course, wonderful, but I had fun finding the exact French window outside which Ambrose lay, and there is a Santana cottage, with its triangular thatched roof, which is either the one Fraulein Funchs lived in, or its replacement.

The Madeira idyll came to an end for Tommy with the war, then with her mother's death in 1924. Her father married Edith Richards, manager of the family's Carmo Hotel, who thus became her hated 'Steppy'. There was more to come. In the 1920s, Alfred and his brother William unwisely diversified beyond their experience, going into banking and commerce with a Portuguese friend and forming an unlimited company, Reid, Castro and Co. When there was a run on the Banco Reid Castro, the whole extended family lost everything – fortune, possessions, property. As the situation had begun to deteriorate, the family moved into three quintas up at Choupana. The main one, Quinta Mirador, is now the Choupana Hills Resort and Spa – still enjoying the unspoilt beauty of Choupana.

With the final crash, Tommy and her husband, Robert 'Taffy' Evans, were left with nothing but a small farm, Quinta Choupana ('Cabin'), that had been a weekend retreat. Nothing daunted, Tommy set to making confectionery and the original cakes known as Bolos de Mel which she would transport down to Funchal to sell. So popular did hers become that they were exported to Fortnum and Mason in London. Isabella de França describes the wild mountain setting 80 years earlier, on 1 March 1854:

We descended a short distance, just here it is not so very steep as lower down, and soon passed the entrance to the Choupana. This quinta is so called from being actually a thatched cottage of a single room, but there are other rooms for all necessary purposes of comfort, though all built separate, each being a detached cottage in itself. We soon left the Rocket Road, turning to the right down a narrow path which becomes more and more rugged, and we had a beautiful view of the ravine on our left ...

The ravine here was magnificent, the foliage was so beautifully green, and the river as it flowed beneath, looked absolutely like a stream of melted silver. Superb rocks rose on each side, winding voltas, or zigzags, between walls of myrtle, laurel, and other trees, with precipices on one side, reminded me of the descent to Rabaçal. I walked some distance on this road, and when tired resumed the rede [hammock].

Today, Tommy's Quinta Choupana belongs to the branch of the Phelps family which returned to Madeira in the 1950s (see p. 32). The whole area is a mass of wonderful walks, linked as it is often via *levadas*, to Terreiro da Luta, Monte, Curral dos Romeiros, the Palheiro Gardens, and the Botanical Gardens.

With the family's misfortune had come not just the end of the Reid empire but the easy life at Bom Sucesso. All that gives you something upon which to ponder as you look down over the fine view of Funchal from the Botanical Gardens where, if you ask, you can see a full copy of Tommy's unpublished typescript and photographs which her daughter, Anne Evans Bohme, presented in 2002. At Reid's Palace (acquired by the Blandy family in 1937 and more recently by the Orient-Express), some of those photographs are on display in the exhibition area and the manuscript will soon be available. There, too, the gardens are lovely and Reid ghosts linger (see also pp. 67–8 and 113–14).

Quinta da Boa Vista

South-east of the Botanical Gardens – though not really walkable – are the gardens at Quinta da Boa Vista, with a special area devoted to orchids grown commercially. The gardens and the orchids are managed by Betty Garton (née Cooke) whose late husband, Cecil, was Honorary British Consul in Madeira. The quinta came into the family's possession at the time of Cecil Garton's great-uncle and the original beauty of the gardens can largely be attributed to Betty's mother-in-law, **Carolina Passos Freitas** (c.1886–1985). The orchids are, however, the work of Betty herself, building on an expertise gained at Wyld Court, her parents' home near Newbury, England. You can buy, as well as admire, the orchids all the year round, though the best show is probably from late November to early May (open Monday to Saturday, 9.00 a.m. – 5.30 p.m.).

Quinta do Palheiro

And so to the gardens of Quinta do Palheiro five miles outside Funchal on the way to Camacha. They are the largest on the island

and the most English in the way they combine the formal and natural. Isabella de França introduces them on 1 September 1853:

We passed the Palheiro de Ferreiro, or Smith's cottage, a splendid seat, built and planted by the late Count Carvalhal, on what was then a bare hill side with the exception of a few old chestnut trees. Perhaps in ancient times a blacksmith might have had his forge on the site, but now it is an extensive park, intersected in all directions by carriage roads, between luxuriant avenues and plantations of various kinds of trees, among which the oaks are remarkable, having been unknown in the Island till introduced by the late Count. The house is small in proportion to the park, but in front of it are the flower gardens, containing many curious plants, and some large tanks with artificial cascades, supplied with water brought down from the higher mountains at a great expense. I regretted not being able to go over these beautiful grounds, but the young Count being absent, and some repairs going on, orders had been given to admit nobody.

Emily Smith had been luckier on 8 December 1841:

We went on horseback to the Palheiro, a Park belonging to Mons Camera de Carvalhal, the richest Fidalgo on the Island. It is in the neighbourhood of Funchal to the East in some Heights & laid out in rides and walks. The house is an ordinary one; the gardens are extensive & remarkable for the double Camellias wh are 14 & 18 feet high, with large white and crimson blossoms in profusion. There are lovely silver Pheasants and Doves — we dined on the grass under the trees.

Fanny Burney Wood adds a useful historical note in March 1839 when she writes of the gardener Count and the struggle between the supporters of the Constitution and those of Dom Miguel (see Queen Maria da Gloria pp. 24–6):

The Count de Carvalhal, notwithstanding his munificence and generosity, was, as a partisan of the young Queen, particularly marked out for vengeance; he took refuge in England, where he remained till 1835.

The Miguelites ransacked his splendid house, destroyed the costly furniture, drank his valuable old wines, injured and cut the trees, shrubs, etc., at his beautiful Country

Seat ... killed or let loose a variety of curious birds and animals kept in the grounds, and in short committed the most wanton depredations upon his property.

Though the gardens had been originally laid out in the eighteenth century by a French landscape gardener, the Count returned from his exile in England with new gardening ideas. The young Count mentioned by Isabella de França had inherited everything in 1837 but was so extravagant that he was eventually forced to sell – the purchaser, in 1884, being John Burden Blandy who built a new and large house on the estate. Elinor Reeder, a keen gardener, married his son, John Ernest Blandy, in 1901, having arrived on the island aboard the United States Navy ship commanded by her admiral father. Florence Du Cane describes the gardens of 1901–1906:

The flower-gardens certainly show no signs of the 'fallen state of things' under their present ownership, and a small enclosed garden a short distance from the house is a perfect treasure-house; though naturally at its best in spring and summer, it is never devoid of flowers. Here English daffodils, pansies, and polyanthuses grow side by side with many a bulb and plant which will just *not* stand the rigours of our English winters. The large-flowered violets, Princess of Wales, and other varieties, flower in their thousands from November till April, with blooms so large that they suggest violas more than violets. Freezias and ixias have seeded themselves in the grass slopes of this little, favoured garden, where the beds are enclosed by trim box hedges. At the corners or angles of the beds the box is cut into all sorts of fancy shapes, such as pyramids and ninepins. In the beds grow large masses of the pale yellow sparaxis, anemones of every shade, single, semi-double, or double, and the graceful little *Cineraria stellata*, in an infinite range of soft colouring. Or a whole bed is devoted to the deep purple *statice*, the beautiful white *Alestroemeria peregrina* or some other chosen flower which gives a definite note to the colour scheme. In March two fine specimens of *Magnolia conspicua* are covered with their cup-like white and lilac blossoms, and stand out in sharp contrast to the deep emerald-green of the *Araucaria braziliensis*, which forms an admirable background to them, and is in itself one of the most beautiful of all trees. Near the magnolias a large shrub of *Cantua buxifolia*, with its bright red tube-like blossoms hanging in graceful bunches, provides a brilliant patch of colour. The lilac *Iris fimbriata*, with its branches of delicately veined flowers, seems to flourish in the shade, and though its individual blossoms are short-lived, they are so freely produced that for many weeks in the late winter and early spring the plants remain in beauty. One could linger for many a long hour in this peaceful spot ...

Mildred Blandy (née Edmonds, 1905–1984), mother of Adam, the present owner, nurtured the gardens during the middle of the last century, creating the sunken garden and rock garden beneath the terrace in front of the house. Mickie, as her close friends called her, was brought up in South Africa by an Irish mother and an English father. In 1934 she married Graham Blandy, having been introduced to him by **Georgina (George) Dalziel**. George had a passion for music and medieval tapestries, which she embroidered. 'Eton-cropped and mannish, sporting a long cigarette-holder', she held court for the Blandy children in a little garden house in Funchal while feeding visiting mice with titbits.

Mildred too had a passion for the arts, particularly poetry, of which she made an anthology that she called 'Hold Happiness Gently', words that are on her tombstone in the British Cemetery (see p. 78). Many of her friends had literary tastes and she played the cello in a Madeira orchestra in the Thirties. As a young woman she contracted tuberculosis and spent a year in a Swiss sanatorium; it was then that she turned to books and letter-writing and gave up the dream of playing tennis for South Africa. Although she was not a natural hostess, she positively enjoyed it when writers, such as Ann Bridge (Lady O'Malley, see pp. 70 and 117), came to stay, heavily underlining the slightest error when she read the resulting book. She found the social obligations that went with marrying the head of a long-established (1811) family business a strain; she dutifully stuck to it, however, and her letters to her sisters in South Africa about Winston and **Clementine Churchill**'s visit to the island in 1950 show that she could rise to, and enjoy, the occasion.

For relief, there was the garden and her gardening correspondents. She exchanged gardening notes with Vita Sackville-West at Sissinghurst Castle and a Japanese camellia expert for years addressed

25. Mildred Blandy at Quinta do Palheiro, courtesy of the family

her as Mr Mildred Blandy. Seeds and cuttings flowed to and fro every week from all over the world. On trips abroad she would smuggle young plants home in her spongebag; plants, of course, thrive when they are filched rather than bought. Among those she introduced to Palheiro and other Madeira gardens were proteas from South Africa, now grown commercially on the island.

Palheiro has always been rather grand. In 1817, before the Blandy days, the Archduchess Leopoldina of Austria, mother of Maria da Gloria of Portugal (see p. 24) passed through Madeira on her way to marry Emperor Pedro I of Brazil. She announced herself dazzled by Palheiro. In 1901, the King and Queen of Portugal, Dom Carlos and **Dona Amélia**, also came on a visit – the Queen lumbering up to Palheiro in a bullock sledge, never a graceful entrance.

When Mildred arrived the quinta was like a multi-faceted Victorian estate: there was the hydraulically-powered sawmill, there were pigs in their sties built from Welsh slate, sheep, cattle, oxen of course, a blacksmith, a creamery, a beekeeper, poultry, an ice-making plant; there were pinewoods and orchards, and the fields supplied vegetables for the market. Every 1 May the gardens would be thrown open to the public and thousands of islanders would flock there with their picnic baskets to laze under the shade of the English oaks bordering the string of pools with their running water. That tradition came to an end but the gardens were then opened to the paying public (open Monday to Friday 10.00 a.m. to 12.30 p.m.).

The gardens are now under the imaginative and unflagging care of Mildred's Swedish daughter-in-law, **Christina Blandy**. The camellias are still as tall as Emily Smith described, and could be the same ones. The peaceful and shady gardens, sporting topiary peacocks, are divided into 'rooms' and more intimate areas such as the *Jardim de Senhora*, the name for which perhaps dates to when women were more confined to their quintas and appreciated their own space.

Christina oversaw, too, the transformation of Count Carvalhal's hunting lodge into a country hotel, the Casa Velha do Palheiro. The farm no longer exists; also in the original quinta grounds are tea rooms and the Palheiro Golf Club.

Departing

It is tempting to linger at Palheiro; but, in the end, perhaps, slightly tongue in cheek (or expatriate tear in eye), we should let Mrs Roundell have her say as she leaves Madeira in 1888:

As, on May 3, we walked down to the beach to embark, the first flowers of the magnolia avenue were just opening their waxen cups, and the gardens were in full beauty. Yet, when we reached England, on May 7, we did not wonder at the eagerness with which the Cape passengers clutched the bunches of wallflowers, primroses, and violets brought on board for sale at Plymouth, and feasted their eyes on the golden gorse and green young larches above Mount Edgcumbe. And when next day we travelled to London, through green fields, past budding hawthorn hedges, banks of primroses and cowslips ... we felt, with irresistible force, that even one wild flower of England was worth all the exotics of Madeira.

To end there would be unfair. It is surely because of visits to places such as Madeira that British gardeners now do their best to grow plants and trees that prefer a milder climate. In our own household we are used to carrying the hibiscus and bougainvillea indoors for the winter, and out again at the end of May. And when my late mother visited us after our return from Madeira, there was an anthurium by her bed, to remind her of the hotel floral arrangements that had so beguiled her.

While visitors may retain and relive in their minds the beauty of Madeira, the experience itself is transitory, so it is worth emphasising the impact of gardens and gardening on the women who lived and live there. Countrywomen worked on their tiny terraced patches, of course, but, until the second half of the twentieth century, opportunities for middle- and upper-class women were limited. With rare exceptions, Portuguese women were confined to home (which included embroidery), family, and convent, but we have sensed that secluded gardens were a space where they could breathe more freely. Luísa Grande (Luzia) made it clear in the early twentieth century that the memory of Madeira's floral grandeur tugged at her when she was away. As for women of mostly British extraction, gardening seems to have been an opportunity for exercise, creativity and fulfilment. And what they created is as lasting and valuable as any other art form.

Madeira Chronology

1300s	Anna d'Arfet (Machim)
1387	Philippa of Lancaster marries João I of Portugal
1425	Dona Constança Rodrigues (Zarco) Chapel of Santa Catarina
1425	birth of Eve and Adam
1450	de França family from Poland
1478	Felipa Moniz (Columbus) d.1480
1492	(or 1488 or 1496) Foundation of Santa Clara Convent by Constança Rodrigues' granddaughters
1533	Felipa (the prophet)
1566	Nuns from Santa Clara to Curral das Freiras
1662	Marriage of Catherine of Braganza
1705–1789	Dona Guiomar de Sá Vilhena
1764	Slave, Amelia, to Leacocks
1765	Protestant Cemetery
1773	Abolition of slavery in Portuguese territories
1786–90	Widow Foster & Son (wine)
1788	Maria Riddell
1803	Floods
1809	Elizabeth Macquarie
1817	Maria Leopoldina of Austria to Palheiro
1819	Elizabeth Dickson (reforestation) m. Joseph Phelps
c.1821	Maria Clementina to Santa Clara Convent
1822	English Church
1823	Sarah Bowdich Lee
1826	Queen Maria da Gloria (d.1853) (1823–34 Miguelite period)

1833	The Hon. Caroline Norton and Mary Young
1838–1839	Fanny Anne Burney (Wood); death of Jane Wood
1838 (Dec.)	Emily Shore (d.June 1839)
1841–43	Emily Genevieve Smith (artist)
1843–52	Catherine Maria Guerin Lowe
1845 fl	Jane Wallas Penfold; Mrs Robley (née Augusta Penfold) (flower publications)
1846	The Misses Rutherford attacked by anti-Kalley mob
1847	Dissension within the English Church comes to a head; Miss Mary Phelps plays the organ
1847–48	Dowager Queen Adelaide
1847	Margaret Dewey (later Reid) and Marchioness Camden
1850	Mariana Xavier da Silva (writer)
1851	Lady Susan Harcourt; Lady Emmeline Stuart-Wortley (December)
1852–62 (fl)	Elizabeth (Bella) Phelps (embroidery)
1853–4	Isabella de França
1853	Death of Princess Maria Amélia of Brazil, aged 21
1859	Archduchess Carlotta; later Empress of Mexico
1860	Empress Elizabeth of Austria (and 1891); Mrs Foote
1862	Opening of Hospício
1866 fl	Fanny Blandy at Quinta de Santa Luzia and Quinta Reveredo
1868–1924	Clara Lawson Reid
1874–1946	Virginia de Castro e Almeida (writer)
1875	Viscondessa Filomena Gabriela Correia Brandão Henriques de Noronha
1875–1945	Luísa Grande (penname, Luzia)
1875 (Jan.)	Marianne North
1876 (July)	Lady (Annie) Brassey (and 1883)
1880	Sarah Forbes Bonetta
1880–1881	Ellen M. Taylor

1880	Sister Mary Jane Wilson; 1884 Foundation of Order; 1891 Santa Cruz; 1907–08 Lazareto; arrested 1910; d.1916
1881–1960	Maria Ana Bianchi Cossart (wine)
1882	(Charlotte) Alice Baker
1884	Quinta do Palheiro purchased by Blandy family
1888 (March)	Julia Anne (Mrs Charles) Roundell
1891	Reid's Palace Hotel; birth of Blanche (Tommy) Reid
1898	Edith Arendrup, school, Santo da Serra
1898–1988	Adelaide Dias Nascimento (Hotel Savoy)
1899 & 1906	Florence and Ella Du Cane
1901	Queen Amélia of Portugal to Palheiro
1902	Flora Shaw Lugard
1910	Revolution; fall of Portuguese monarchy; republic; religious communities closed; Sister Wilson expelled
1914	Katherine Routledge
1921	Ex-Empress Zita of Austria
c.1928	J(essie) Edith Hutcheon and Dame Henrietta Barnett
1930	Martha Teles (artist) born
1934	Mildred Blandy joins family at Quinta do Palheiro
1951–52	Elizabeth Nicholas
1952	Greta Monica Phelps
1953	Cecilia Rose Zino Foundation
1969	Ann Bridge
1972	Manuela de Freitas (wine)
1974	Portuguese Revolution
1976	Autonomy for Madeira

Madeira Bibliography

Women's Works

Baker, C. Alice, *A Summer in the Azores with a Glimpse of Madeira* (Boston, Lee and Shepard, 1882)

Barros, Bernadette, *Donna de Sá Vilheno: Uma Mulher do Sécolo XVIII* (Funchal, Centro de Estudos de História do Atlântico, 2001)

Bowdich, T. Edward, *Excursions in Madeira and Porto Santo during the Autumn of 1823 ... To which is added by Mrs Bowdich* (London, George B. Whittaker, 1825)

Brassey, Lady, *A Voyage in the 'Sunbeam': Our Home on the Ocean for Eleven Months* (London, Longmans Green, 1899)

Brassey, Lady, *In the Trades, the Tropics and the Roaring Forties* (London, Longmans Green, 1885)

Bridge, Ann and Lowndes, Susan, *A Selective Traveller in Portugal* (London, Chatto and Windus, 1958; 1st edition 1949)

Bridge, Ann, *The Malady in Madeira* (New York, McGraw Hill, 1969)

Carlotta, Archduchess, *Un Hiver à Madère* (Vienna, 1863)

Cust, Mrs Henry, *Wanderers: Episodes from the Travels of Lady Emmeline Stuart-Wortley and Her Daughter Victoria 1849–1855* (London, Jonathan Cape, 1927)

Du Cane, Florence, *The Flowers and Gardens of Madeira*, with illustrations by Ella Du Cane (London, A. and C. Black, 1926; 1st edition 1909)

Dunphy, Terry, *The Invincible Victorian: The Life of Mary Jane Wilson* (Whitchurch?, Franciscan Sisters of Our Lady of Victories, c.1950)

Fernando, Abel Soares, *Mary Jane Wilson: Roeteiro* (Funchal, Congregação das Irmãs Franciscanas de Nossa Senhora das Vitórias, 2003)

Foote, Mrs, *Recollections of Central America and the West Coast of Africa* (London, 1869)

de França, Isabella, *Journal of a Visit to Madeira and Portugal 1853–1854* (Funchal, Junta Geral do Distrito Autónomo do Funchal, 1970)

Gates, Barbara Timm (ed.), *Journal of Emily Shore* (Charlottesville, University of Virginia Press, 1991)

Harcourt, Lady Susan Vernon, *Sketches in Madeira: Drawn from Nature and on Stone* (London, Thomas McLean, 1851)

Hutcheon, J. Edith, *Things Seen in Madeira: A Description of One of the Most Beautiful Islands in the World etc.* (London, Seely, 1928)

Lamas, Maria 'Quintas Madeirenses' in *Arquipélago da Madeira: Maravilha Atlântica* (Funchal, Editorial ECO, 1956)

Lowe, R.T., Norton, the Hon. C.E.C., and Young, M., *A History of the Fishes of Madeira* (London, John Van Voorst, 1843–60)

Milward, Richard, *Triumph Over Tragedy: The Life of Edith Arendrup, a Victorian Courtauld 1846–1943* (Merton, Priory Press, 1991)

Nicholas, Elizabeth, *Madeira and the Canaries: A Traveller's Notebook* (London, Hamish Hamilton, 1953)

North, Marianne, *Recollections of a Happy Life*, 2 vols (London, Macmillan, 1893)

Norton, Caroline, *A Woman's Reward* (London, Saunders & Otley, 1835)

Penfold, Jane Wallas, *Madeira: Flowers, Fruits and Ferns* (London, Reeve Bros, 1845)

Ribeiro, Abilo Pina, *Sister Wilson Story* (Portugal, Franciscan Sisters of Our Lady of Victories, 1993)

R[iddell], Maria, *Voyage to the Madeira etc Isles* (Salem, N. Coverly, 1802; 1st edition 1792)

Robley, Augusta J., *A Selection of Madeira Flowers* (London, Reeve Bros, 1845)

Rolt, Margaret S., *A Great-Niece's Journals: Being Extracts from the Journals of Fanny Anne Burney (Mrs Wood)* (London, Constable, 1926)

Roundell, Mrs Charles, *A Visit to the Azores with a Chapter on Madeira* (London, Bickers, 1889)

Routledge, Katherine, *The Mystery of Easter Island* (Illinois, Adventures Unlimited Press, 1998; first published 1919)

Shore, Emily, *Journal of Emily Shore* (London, Kegan Paul, 1898; 1st edition 1891)

Shore, Louisa, *Elegies and Memorials* (London, Kegan Paul, 1890)

Smith, Mrs Reginald, *A Panoramic View of the City of Funchal* (London, 1844)

Stuart-Wortley, Lady Emmeline, *A Visit to Portugal and Madeira* (London, Chapman Hall, 1854)

Taylor, Ellen M, *Madeira: Its Scenery and How to See It, with Letters of a Year's Residence* (London, Edward Stanford, 1882; 2nd edition 1889)

Unpublished Manuscripts and Drawings

Evans, Blanche Reid (Tommy), 'Reids Hotels and the Reids at Home', in possession of the family; can be seen at Reid's Hotel or the Botanical Gardens, Funchal

Macquarie, Elizabeth, '1809 Journal'; www.chnm.gmu.edu/worldhistorysources, 'Journeys in Time', The Journals of Elizabeth Macquarie 1809–1822, Mitchell Library, Sydney

Phelps, Mary, Diaries 1839–1843 (IV/195/26/1–3 (typescripts)) Mss Noel Cossart Collection, Lambeth Archives, Minet Library

Smith, Emily Genevieve, 1841 Diary (D/500/2), Dorset Record Office, Dorchester

Smith, Emily Genevieve, Folio of drawings, Quinta das Cruzes Museum, Funchal

General Reference

Adams, Joseph, *An Account of the Lazaretto in the Island of Madeira* (London, Smith & Sons, 1806)

Anon., *An Historical Sketch of the Island of Madeira* (London, 1819)

Bowles, William Lisle, *The Spirit of Discovery* (Bath, 1804)

Bryans, *Madeira: Pearl of the Atlantic* (London, Robert Hale, n.d.)

Burke's Genealogical Peerage ..., P. Townsend (ed.) (105th edition, 1970)

Cabral do Nascimento, João, *A Madeira* (Lisbon, c.1958)

Chedzoy, Alan, *Scandalous Woman* (London, Alison & Busby, 1992)

Camden, Viscount, *The British Chaplaincy in Madeira* (London, 1847)

Clode, Luiz Peter, *Registo Bio-bibliográfico de Madeirenses: secs XIX e XX* (Funchal, Caixa Economica do Funchal, 198?)

Cossart, Noel, see Mansell-Jones

Croft-Cooke, Rupert, *Madeira* [Wine], (London, Putnam, 1961)

Dictionary of National Biography

Gonçalves, Ernesto, 'Rua da Mouraria ou a Aventura Duma Palavra' in *Arquivo Histórico da Madeira*, vol. X, 1958

Gregory, Desmond, *The Beneficent Usurpers: A History of the British in Madeira* (London, University Presses, 1988)

Harcourt, Edward Vernon, *A Sketch of Madeira: Containing Information for the Traveller, or Invalid Visitor* (London, John Murray, 1851)

Hopkirk, Mary, *Queen Adelaide* (London, John Murray, 1946)

Koebel, William, *Madeira Old and New* (London, Francis Griffiths, 1909)

Lethbridge, Alan, *Madeira: Impressions and Associations* (London, Methuen, 1924)

Liddell, Alex, *Madeira* [wine] (London, Faber & Faber, 1998)

Mansell-Jones, Penelope (ed.), *The Island Vineyard* (Noel Cossart) (London, Christie's Wine Publications, 1984)

Nash, Roy, *Scandal in Madeira* (Lewes, Sussex, The Book Guild, 1990)

Newell, Herbert, *The English Church in Madeira ...: A History* (Oxford, Oxford University Press, 1931)

Rendell, J.M., *Concise Handbook of the Island of Madeira* (London, Kegan Paul, 1881)

Vieira, Alberto and Clode, Francisco, *The Sugar Route in Madeira* (Funchal, Associação das Refinadores de Açucar Portugueses, 1996)

Viera, Alberto, 'Slavery in Madeira in the XV and XVII Centuries: The Balance' (Funchal, Centro Estudos História Atlântico; 1997)

Viera, Alberto, 'Slaves With or Without Sugar, Madeira's Case' (Funchal, Centro Estudos História Atlântico, 1997)

Weaver, H.J., *Reid's Hotel* (London, Souvenir, 1991)

Modern Travel Guides

Bolt, Rodney, *Madeira & Porto Santo* (London, Cadogan Guides, 2003)

Catling, Christopher, *Madeira* (Windsor, Berkshire, AA Essential, 2001)

Farrow, John and Susan, *Madeira: A Complete Guide* (London, Robert Hale, 1994)

Hancock, Matthew, *Rough Guide to Madeira* (London, Rough Guides, 2001)

Quintal, Raimundo, *Levadas and Footpaths of Madeira* (Funchal, Francisco Ribeiro, 2002)

Rice, Christopher and Melanie, *Madeira* (London, New Holland, Globetrotter, 2003)

Sale, Richard, *Madeira* (Ashbourne, Derbyshire, Landmark, 1999)

Underwood, John and Pat, *Landscapes of Madeira: A Countryside Guide* (Exeter, Sunflower Books, 2002)

Index

Look for categories such as: artists, chapels and churches, convents, gardens, gardeners, hotels, museums, Orders (religious), quintas, rivers, sculptures, streets etc, wine companies. Husbands are mostly indexed with wives or family.